Countering Antisemitism & Hate

Countering Antisemitism and Hate: A How-To Guide for Youth (8-18), Family and Educators

ISBN (paperback): 978-1-963271-07-2
ISBN (Ebook): 978-1-963271-08-9

ARMINLEAR

Armin Lear Press, Inc.
215 W Riverside Drive, #4362
Estes Park, CO 80517

Countering Antisemitism & Hate

A How-To Guide for Youth (8-18), Family and Educators

Lynne Azarchi & Harlene Lichter Galen

ARMINLEAR

If you will it, it is no dream.

—Theodor Herzl

The world will not be destroyed by those who do evil, but by those who watch and do nothing.

—Albert Einstein

In a place where no one behaves like a human being, you must strive to be human.

—Hillel, *Pirkei Avot*

Note from the Authors

We wrote this guide *before* the October 7, 2023 War between Israel and Hamas began—and we are reeling from all the pain, death, trauma, torture, and suffering that Israelis, the hostages and prisoners, and the Palestinians are suffering. We are praying that there will be an end to the War soon and that peace, for all peoples, will be the solution.

For millennia, Jews have been victimized by antisemitism. Now in 2024, antisemitism for both adults and youth is rising to new all-time records.

As Jewish parents ourselves, we realize that other Jewish parents and teachers are afraid. Overall, our culture has evolved to "Shhhhhhhhh. Don't make a fuss" in order to keep safe.

However, today we have a unique opportunity to create a paradigm shift for our children—to teach them to **safely** push back and defend themselves. Because we know we need to prepare our children earlier, the guidebook begins with information for building a foundation of Jewish pride and identity through basic concepts appropriate for even elementary schoolers. Next we present calming strategies for peer interaction. Safe approaches to fortify our children to "stand up and speak out" and pointers on reporting to a trusted adult follow. Currently, antisemitism is at record-breaking heights on college and university campuses. Let's heed the need to prepare our children to stop the cycles of hate, tropes and stereotypes *before* they arrive at college.

As staunch believers in *Tikkun Olam*, Jews also have the responsibility of "repairing the world." So, we are obligated to report both antisemitism and other biases in schools, workplaces and in our communities. Hatemongers and bullies need to learn consequences and boundaries.

Jewish adults have one additional duty—to role model courage and persistence in building a culture of repelling and thwarting antisemitism. Then when our children are adults, they will have a better chance of commanding more kindness and respect, and living openly and proudly with others as Jews.

* * *

"Insofar as one of the major battlefronts has indeed become educational settings, it's vital that our children and grandchildren are as prepared as possible for what they may face. Not easy under any circumstance. When it comes to affirming Jewish identity, Zionism, and pro-Israelism, it can require not just confidence in the facts, but also a heavy dose of social courage. That's why if we count on young people to stand up and be heard, then we have to help prepare them for the various situations in which they may find themselves. Plus, they need to feel the support of family, Jewish organizations, and Jewish institutions on campus."
—**David Harris,** former CEO, American Jewish Committee

Contents

Part One

Acknowledging the Jewish Elephant in the Room

Introduction
A. Antisemitism Threatens Our Youth

> My teacher said she could not tell I was Jewish; it did not feel good to hear that.
> **—Sophie, fifth grader**

> No one at school knows about my religion and culture and it makes me feel alone.
> **—Jake, sixth grader**

> Someone threw pennies at me and the other kids laughed in the hall. I turned away and felt embarrassed. I didn't know what to do and told no one.
> **—Gabe, seventh grader**

> My girlfriends said I couldn't be Jewish because I had blue eyes and blond hair. This came out of nowhere and I didn't know how to respond. I told my parents, but they told me, "Just let it go."
> **—Rebecca, ninth grader**

In ninth grade, I was called a "dirty Jew" by a classmate. In 10th grade, I was told I should have died in the Holocaust with the rest of my family, and in 11th grade, I was told that Zionism was racism and that we were colonial settlers.
—Leah, high school junior

I was very angry, but I tried to contain my anger. I talked with the leaders of the Jewish union at my school, and we made plans to speak to the entire high school about what was happening in Israel, Sadly, we were never able to do that.
—Noah, high school senior

We really don't know how to stop antisemitism and I am nervous to go to college next year.
—Zach, high school senior

And here's a quote issued by the Students for Justice in Palestine posted on October 8, 2023 after the October 7th massacre in Israel:

> "The events that took place yesterday are a step towards a free Palestine . . . freedom is not a matter of if but when. We stand in solidarity with Palestinian resistance fighters."
>
> University of Virginia Chapter, Students for Justice in Palestine (the largest anti-Israel student group in the United States.)

How does it feel knowing that Jewish youth are being targeted for no other reason except their religion? How does it feel to send children to what should be the safe space of school and realize it is actually not safe?

We can do something powerful right now that will cast ripples of positivity and counter antisemitism not only immediately, but for years to come. How? Better educating our children, tweens, and teens.

Noah, the high school senior, beseeches us, "The new generation must be educated and our voices must be heard."

If we wait until today's youth become adults, it will be too late. If parents and teachers persist in ducking our collective heads in the sand, our children and teens will continue to suffer the demeaning sting of antisemitism, harm or even destroying their pride and self-esteem.

Those of us who are parents and grandparents need to do our part to move ourselves and others along the continuum from ignorance to tolerance and inclusion.

How much work do we need to do? Is an in-depth approach a must? Take the following quiz and discover.

B. Do You and Your Children/Teens Need This Book?

1. If your child heard an antisemitic expression like "dirty Jew," or "Jews control the banks and the media," they would:

   a. Do nothing

   b. Tell me

   c. Not tell me

   d. Tell the perpetrator that wasn't nice

   e. I have no idea

2. If your teen heard that the Holocaust never happened, they would:

   a. Do nothing

   b. Tell a friend

   c. Tell a Jewish friend

   d. Tell a teacher

   e. Tell me

   f. I have no idea

3. If your child heard "Jews are cheap" or the term "Jew bastards," they would:

   a. Do nothing

   b. Tell an adult

   c. I have no idea

   d. Realize the antisemitism, but pretend not to hear it

4. If your child watched kids pull off a Muslim girl's hijab, they would:

   a. Do nothing

   b. Tell an adult

   c. I have no idea

   d. Console the child

5. If your child heard a stereotype like "all Asians are smart," they would:

   a. Do nothing

   b. Tell an adult

   c. I have no idea

   d. Realize it is a stereotype and say so

6. Based on the Jewish tradition of *tikkun olam*, is your child inspired to "repair the world" (give back) in any of the following ways?

   a. Community service—for example, volunteering for soup kitchens or visiting Jewish elderly

   b. Create a fundraiser or be on a fundraising team to help those who have less

   c. Join a group and be a contributing member of a team that, for example, fights antisemitism or works for social justice or human rights

   d. Stand up for those who can't stand up for themselves, such as a child being teased or bullied for their religion, gender orientation, ethnicity, or appearance

Did you know how your child would respond to these six situations? If not, consider this an eye-opener: You are a member of the culture of bystanders. But you can become an active opponent of antisemitism and hate—and this guidebook can be your ally.

Section I

Disrupt the Jewish Culture of Bystanders

A creative, thoughtful, and accomplished people such as the Jewish people should be known by what they have done and not by what has been done to them.
—Deborah Lipstadt, author of ***Antisemitism: Here and Now***; Ambassador, U.S. Special Envoy to Monitor and Combat Antisemitism

A. Antisemitism—A Surging Problem

As a Jewish people, we are only 0.2 percent of the world's population and yet endure bias and hate disproportionate to numbers and have endured these for centuries (see Resources).

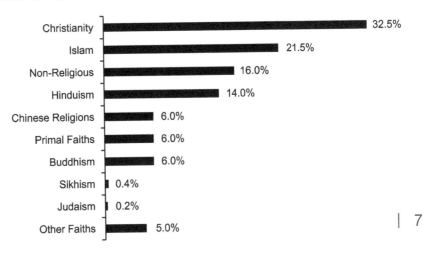

Tragically, antisemitism is spiking once again. Many people are radicalized and are conducting acts of hate, bullying and crime on Jews. Other religious and ethnic minorities are also experiencing an increase in hate and discrimination.

The BBC reported "a nearly 7% rise in religion-based hate crime, with a 14% increase in crimes targeting Jews or Jewish institutions" in the United States in 2020.[1] Teachers in the classroom "noted a disturbing uptick in incidents involving swastikas, derogatory language, Nazi salutes, and Confederate flags."[2]

There were historically high levels of antisemitic incidents nationwide in 2020, with 2,024 incidents of assault, harassment, and vandalism reported to the Anti-Defamation League (ADL).[3] Two years later, the totals were far worse, reaching 3,697 antisemitic incidents, or 83 percent higher. It marked the third time in a five-year period that the year-end total was the highest ever recorded.[4]

Incidents increased in categories including antisemitic harassment (up 29 percent to 2,298); antisemitic vandalism (up 51 percent to 1,288), and antisemitic assaults (up 26 percent to 111). One person was killed. Visibly Orthodox Jews were targeted in 53 percent of the assaults.[5]

The ADL reported that the dramatic increases could not be attributed to any one cause or ideology. Many, however, were attributed to organized white supremacist propaganda activity (102 percent increase to 852 incidents). Incidents were up sharply in K–12 schools and college campuses, as well as attacks on Orthodox Jews. There were also ninety-one bomb threats toward Jewish institutions.[6]

One of the best recent reports on antisemitism was undertaken by the American Jewish Committee (AJC), the leading global Jewish advocacy organization (Lynne is a Board member for AJC's NJ chapter). In this report—the *2022 State of Antisemitism in America*—we learn that nine in ten American Jews believe antisemitism to be a problem in the United States today and that some Jews are changing their behavior out of fear, such as not displaying publicly that they are Jewish, attending Jewish events, or going to synagogue.[7]

A 2022 AJC survey of Jewish millennials broadened to include anti-Israelism. The survey revealed the following:

- 28 percent of American Jewish millennials reported that the anti-Israel climate, on campus and elsewhere, made them rethink their commitment to Israel

- 23 percent of American Jewish millennials said they were forced to hide their Jewish identity because of an anti-Israel climate on campus and elsewhere[8]

Why Do These Data Raise an Urgent Issue for Your Family?

Whether it's today, tomorrow, next month, or next year, your children will hear antisemitic, biased statements or stereotypes. Someone might even physically threaten them because of their Jewishness. Never forget that history repeats. Perhaps, buried in your own memories, is a well-guarded *ouch* similar to the authors' remembrances:

Lynne and Harlene will never forget their first bitter taste of antisemitism. Even these many decades afterward, the hurt persists.

Lynne:

> As I wrote in my 2020 book *The Empathy Advantage*: *Coaching Children to be Kind, Respectful and Successful:*

> "No one wants to be the 'other.' No one wants to be an outsider or made to feel small. It happens to everyone at one stage of life or another. It took a while for me to suffer that first awful experience."

> "As a Jewish kid growing up in a small, largely Italian-Catholic community in [Trenton, New Jersey's] Chambersburg section, I remember visiting a friend's house when I was in ninth grade and accidentally overhearing my friend's parents chatting in the kitchen. Out of nowhere, I heard the remark: "Well, you know the Jews killed Christ.""

> "I was thunderstruck; I'd never been exposed to that thinking before. It was a shock that these adults, whom I valued and respected, thought Jewish people were responsible for killing their Lord. I instantly felt like a bit of an outsider in my friend's home. From then on, I was on alert for remarks

wherever I went: in the supermarket, in the movies, in restaurants. It was disheartening—and a wakeup call."[9]

"Yes, I was the 'other.' Another memory that didn't make it into my book was my father being 'othered' to the point of being assaulted. Yes, growing up in Trenton in the 1930s, he was beaten up for being Jewish. He was constantly chased and bullied. He told me the only safe place he could find was the Trenton YMHA, a facility for Jewish youth."

Harlene:

Unlike Lynne, I was initiated into "the other" life in my early childhood. My dad, Sam Lichter, was a beginning lawyer in Pittsburgh. Money was tight, so Dad used his creativity. He did a form of bartering with his clients, providing them legal services for whatever they were able to offer in return. One client paid by giving Dad a small lot in a suburb; other barter payments resulted in a little house on the lot. My family moved into it a few weeks before I was five, old enough to attend public school. Ours was the only Jewish family in the neighborhood. When children asked my name, I always answered with both my first and last names.

For about a week, my mother, Bea, walked with me the five blocks to school. I couldn't wait until she let me walk with all the other kids without her.

That day finally came. I was so excited that I was the first one to start walking. As other children came up behind me, I heard words. Initially, I thought they were saying "Harlene Lichter," and I smiled because I thought they were calling me. The words got loud and louder still, and then I clearly heard what they were saying: "Dirty Jew Liquor Dirty Jew Liquor Dirty Jew Liquor" repeatedly for many blocks until we reached the school doors.

B. Jewish Youth—Unprepared and Suffering

Citizens are not born, but made.
—**Baruch Spinoza,** Jewish philosopher

Baruch Spinoza speaks to us from the seventeenth century, advocating that we mold our future citizens with care. Could our failure to heed his advice be the answer to the troubling question of why, when our sons and daughters leave our home for college or jobs, they are so unprepared for antisemitism?

Let's take a minute and walk in the shoes of Jewish college students. Unprepared and having no training in anti-bias, they expect belonging and inclusion. Instead, they encounter exclusion, hate, antisemitism, and anti-Israel sentiment—an unexpected brick wall.

Rabbi Michael Lerner, a political activist, says young Jews don't understand the historical context surrounding antisemitism. Regarding his lectures at campuses around the United States, he says, "I've met thousands of young Jews who never learned or have conveniently forgotten the realities of their own history."[10]

In his book, *Jewish Pride,* author Ben M. Freeman expands on Lerner's observations: "What Lerner is suggesting is that certain young progressive light-skinned Jews have forgotten the cyclical nature of violent [antisemitism] faced by their own ancestors and have started seeing themselves as privileged white people whose only role in the progressive world is to support other communities in their fights against oppression."[11]

ANTI-SEMITIC BYSTANDER
PIPELINE FOR YOUTH

PRE-SCHOOL	ELEMENTARY SCHOOL	MIDDLE SCHOOL	HIGH SCHOOL
"My friend told me Jews can't get into heaven."	"Pick up the pennies. Aren't you Jewish?"	"I heard the Holocaust never happened."	"Israel is an Apartheid state."

RACISM

The point is that if our college students are unprepared for antisemitism, then our high schoolers are also unprepared. If our high schoolers are unprepared, then so are our middle schoolers, and so on and so on. It's a pipeline of unpreparedness.

C. Bystanders—Problems vs. Solutions

Most of us talk about name-calling, offensive jokes, tropes and exclusion that we've encountered. However, we fail to discuss *how to deal effectively* with these problems. As a community, Jews have their priorities backward. We dwell on the problems, not the solutions. We live in a bystander society.

Being a target causes emotional and psychological harm. Furthermore, a bystander who witnesses bias and bullying and feels powerless suffers psychological consequences.[12]

As bystanders, we succumb to group or societal pressure. From an early age, we are compromised, fearful to express our opinion, frightened to intervene, and afraid to get involved. Mean and aggressive people are scary, and we figuratively and literally look down at the floor cowering as bullies rise to power. We are conflict avoiders.

You can see from the chart below that bystanders are in the majority, letting those who bully and demean dominate the culture—whether it's at a social gathering or in the classroom or office.

Type of Involvement in Bullying Activities

When Jewish children and teens face antisemitism, what do they do? Mostly nothing. Unprepared, without practiced strategies or tactics for responding, they remain victims and targets. Compounding the problem, most Jewish children are afraid to share these bias incidents with their teachers or parents—even in the face of safety issues! In some instances, Jewish parents have coached their children not to draw attention to themselves or make a fuss. This strategy allows the perpetrators and bullies to flourish.

Many Jewish people have inherited the culture of conflict avoidance, which is a hallmark of a bystander society. Addressing conflict is stressful, so both adults and youth look the other way. However, harm still lurks. Conflicts don't disappear. Thoughtful Jewish adults realize they need to push back.

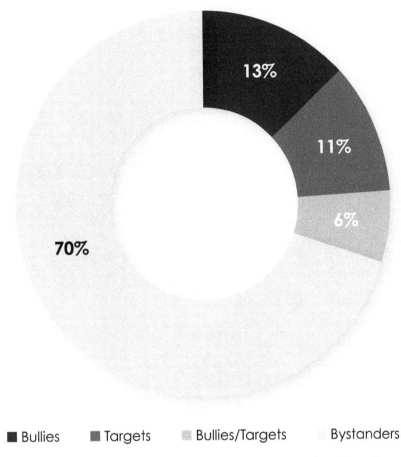

13%

11%

6%

70%

■ Bullies ■ Targets ▨ Bullies/Targets ░ Bystanders

Source: Tonia R. Nansel, Mary Overpeck, Ramani S. Pilla, W. June Ruan, Bruce Simons-Morton, and Peter Scheidt, "Bullying Behaviors Among US Youth Prevalence and Association with Psychosocial Adjustment," *Journal of the American Medical Association* 285, no. 16 (2001), doi:10.1001/jama.285.16.2094.

Adults wish they had the courage to jump in and tell haters, name-callers, and those who are biased that their rhetoric and vitriol are unacceptable. They admit that our children need to be better prepared for antisemitism. They urgently feel that when our youth encounter a safety issue, they need to tell an adult who is equipped to help them.

Take heart! Inaction is *not* the parents' and educators' fault.

Why? They are uninformed how to handle the offenses. However, with this guidebook, the reader can turn from problems to discovering research-informed, developmentally appropriate, and evidence-based solutions, strategies, and tactics for Jewish youth— many of whom at this very moment are enduring daily and rising episodes of antisemitism.

Section II

Explore Jewish History, Including the Holocaust, to Build Identity, Values, and Pride

Courage is never to let your actions be influenced by your fears.
—**Arthur Koestler,** British Jewish author and journalist, 1905–1983

A. Identity—Definition, Importance, Early Start in Strengthening

Definition

Identity refers to a child's discovery of "Who I Am." Identity includes different components such as abilities, ethnicity, gender, sexual orientation, religion, and race that together form a whole person. Renowned psychologist Erik Erikson reminds us that a healthy identity requires both an individual's personally satisfying, multifaceted, coherent sense of self and the surrounding community's recognition and affirmation of this sense.[13]

Importance

Learning about Jewish history and culture strengthens Jewish identity. Rabbi Kerry M. Olitzky, educator, administrator, and prolific author, advises, "One of the chief lessons of Jewish parenting wisdom is the importance of sharing Jewish identity for your children by creating Jewish memories."[14]

In his advocacy for Jewish pride, author Ben Freeman touts identity's worth. "The reason why identity is important, particularly when you are a minority, is that defining your own identity is to state your personal and communal right to self-determination," he says.[15]

Early Start in Strengthening Identity

Research informs us that a child starts to develop ethnic self-identity at age three. But giving children the foundation for Jewish identity can start even earlier in both direct and indirect ways. An example of the direct way is how babies and toddlers can respond to a parent's singing of the Shema prayer as part of the nightly bedtime routine; gradually, most begin to sing along. An example of the indirect way is celebrating Jewish life and participating in the Jewish community through sharing books from PJ Library (see Resources). The books provide opportunities for adults to talk to their kids about Jewish values and traditions.[16]

An early start doesn't guarantee that youth will immediately feel comfortable with their identity. Lynne's identity challenge is common: She hid her identity for many years, afraid to let peers know she was Jewish. Reaching thirteen was a turning point. Preparing for her bat mitzvah, she was enthralled with Emma Lazarus, the poet, writer, and social worker who welcomed thousands of Jewish immigrants to New York City in the late 1800s. You know Lazarus from her poem inscribed at the base of the Statue of Liberty:

> Give me your tired, your poor,
> your huddled masses yearning to breathe free,
> The wretched refuse of your teeming shore.
> Send these, the homeless, tempest-tost to me.
> I lift my lamp beside the golden door.

Lazarus was a Jewish heroine with whom Lynne connected and honored in her bat mitzvah speech. Lynne saved her bat mitzvah script and it inspires her to this day. (Lynne memorized the Lazarus poem, and so can your kids.)

B. Values—History and Individual Choices

When we give children clear and consistent messages about what is important through what we say and do, they are more likely to be inspired to act on those values—and become adults who draw on the rich and enduring principles of Judaism to build a meaningful and fulfilling life. [17]

History

Historians agree that Judaism is based on six core values that are all embedded in the Torah. Jews have relied on these six values as a compass since ancient times. They are the value of life, world peace, justice and equality, access to education for all, family, and social responsibility. Undergirding these six values is monotheism, the belief in one God affirmed in the Shema: "Hear, O Israel. The Lord our God. The Lord is One." Traditionally, Jews are seen as being responsible for living daily in a manner that models these values for others as part of a covenant God made with the Jewish people.

Fulfilling this unique responsibility of what is often called spreading the light has been a struggle for Jews. Four thousand years ago, the struggle was great because non-Jewish society's ways of living were diametrically opposed to Jewish beliefs. As millennia passed, gradual acceptance of Judaism's six values began to occur among other societies, but the struggle continues. [18]

Individual Choices

Free choice plays a role in which Jewish values are emphasized by people at different periods of their lives. During Lynne's childhood and teen years, two values rose to the top in her home—*tikkun olam*—a component of social responsibility—and education. It wasn't just education. It was "education, education, education," like a mantra. Then, throughout adulthood, not only *tikkun olam* but other facets of social responsibility received greater amounts of attention as she went on to serve on the boards of many Jewish nonprofits.

Growing up, Harlene sought to focus on justice and equality through projects with the Girl Scouts and volunteering for marginalized groups' causes. As she became more mature, her experiences as a teacher and parent elevated the value of family to a place of primary commitment.

Hidden in the lives of earlier generations in your own family are examples of Jewish values that relatives chose to accentuate. Dig a little deeply and you may discover some that have long-term meaning for your children. Here's one "find" that Harlene's three kids marked as a keeper about their great-great-uncles' testament to their survival skills as Jews. In the 1850s, the Salzburg branch of her family lived in Pren in what is now Lithuania, but then was part of Russia. Typical of how the Russian military filled its quota, the three youngest brothers—ten-year-old Wolfe, nine-year-old Harris, and five-year-old Simon Salzburg—were kidnapped from the yeshiva where they were attending school and brought to a military encampment to be conscripted into the Russian army. On a dark night, the three oldest brothers—Louis, Joseph, and David—rode on horseback to the encampment, snatched their younger siblings, and galloped off before the soldiers could figure out what happened. The six brothers stayed in hiding until they could go home safely.

C. Pride—*Nachat/Nachas*

Pessimism and negativity about being Jewish are clear factors in dissuading young Jews from following their heritage. Who wants to be a perpetual victim? We suggest that you introduce your Jewish children to the *nachat/nachas* antidote! (Nachat is Hebrew for tranquility and contentment; nachas, its Yiddish cousin, refers to the joy and pride felt from the accomplishments and successes of others, especially loved ones.)

Help your youth celebrate belonging to the Jewish people, who represent only one-fifth of 1 percent of the world population yet have consistently advanced the frontiers of worldwide civilization, including receiving 22.4 percent of all Nobel Prizes through 2020 (208 of 930).[19]

Share the Jews' transforming contributions to globally defending human dignity and the advancement of human rights over three millennia. Encourage the new generation to be amazed at the miraculous Jewish determination to persevere against unimaginable challenges without ever abandoning hope for a more just future.

Telling your offspring about your own explorations of Jewish pride, like those of Lynne and Harlene, may be an even more effective model.

Lynne:

I heard about Reza Aslan's history book *Zealot: The Life and Times of Jesus of Nazareth* and thought it would be interesting to read about biblical times from a Muslim point of view. What a journey!

Jews were assailed by the Assyrians and survived. Next came the Babylonians, who marched the Hebrew tribes to Iraq. Surprisingly, Jews not only survived but returned to Israel.

Next, the Greeks and the Romans killed and plundered Jews, who were a minority. How is it that there are any Jews left today after centuries of death and murder (not to mention the Holocaust)?

That is the miracle—even greater than the miracle of Hanukkah. *We survived!* Thousands of years of persecution and we are still here.

Harlene:

My exploration of different individual's views on dealing with antisemitism introduced me to Ben M. Freeman's thinking in his book *Jewish Pride: Rebuilding a People* and my personal discovery of a broader Jewish pride: "As individuals we may base our Jewish pride on our own unique perspectives, but our pride is also collective. It belongs to us all as a people and it binds us each to the rest of the Jewish community."[20]

In Freeman's book, I gained awareness that despite distinct differences, common characteristics are embedded in the four main Diasporic Jewish communities: 1) my own Ashkenazi (central and eastern Europe), 2) Bera-Yisrael (Ethiopia), 3) Mizrahi (Middle East or North Africa), and 4) Sephardic (initially the Iberian Peninsula and, due to expulsion, later the Mediterranean, parts of Europe, North Africa, the Middle East, and the Balkans), as well as in smaller Jewish communities in China and India. All six sparkle with their own variety of resilience, advocacy for themselves, support for the country of Israel, rich cultural traditions, and contributions to the wider world. What a meaningful and powerful expansion of my personal Jewish pride when I discovered collective pride!

As Freeman wrote, "We must celebrate the incredible diversity in our community, heal where we need healing—and above all, know that, despite our differences, we are one people."[21]

D. Positive Lessons from the Holocaust

We know the Jews of the Holocaust as victims, marched into cattle cars. "Why didn't they do something?" we cry with exasperation. Germans, Austrians, and Poles as bystanders looked the other way.

But surprise, surprise. There *were* Jewish resisters called partisans, both men and women, who fought against the Nazis—more than thirty thousand, according to recent sources. The Warsaw Uprising, a personal inspiration for us, is a story of courage and resilience in the Jewish ghetto (see Activities section for more on Jewish heroism). We strongly recommend the book *MILA 18* by Leon Uris, a historical novel about German-occupied Poland. Many stories and films are just coming forward now, some in webinar and pod-cast form. They are a must-share with your family or classroom to learn about Jews who fought back (see Resources).

Most European countries were overrun and dictated to by the Third Reich. Laudable exceptions were Denmark and Albania. In Denmark, almost eight thousand Jews escaped to neutral Sweden, defying the Third Reich's death sentence.

* * *

Whoever saves a single life is as if one saves the entire world.
—**Talmud**

* * *

Here in the United States, perhaps the least known of heroic rescuers are the "Righteous Among the Nations," non-Jews like Jan Karski and Irena Sendler who risked their lives to save Jews during the Holocaust. Their empathy and action for justice took many forms, including hiding Jews in barns, attics, and cellars; supplying forged identity papers; and sharing their own meager supply of food.

Lynne was lucky to travel to Poland on an AJC mission in 2015. Her visit to the POLIN Museum of the History of Polish Jews in Warsaw, which detailed centuries of European antisemitism starting in the year 1000, was a rude awakening.

More horrifying was her visit to the Auschwitz and Belzec death camps. She is fairly certain most of her relatives were killed in these two camps—her father's side from Belarus and Ukraine in Belzec, her mother's side from Poland in Auschwitz. But she did leave with some positives.

On her trip to Poland, Lynne spent time at a memorial and museum dedicated to Jozef and Wiktonia Ulma. These non-Jews from Markowa followed their hearts and coura- geously hid two Jewish families in their homes. Tragically, they were all discovered, and the Ulma family and the Jewish families they were protecting, including the children, were executed by the German police.

Yad Vashem: The World Holocaust Remembrance Center in Israel embarked on a world- wide project to pay tribute to 'The Righteous Among the Nations' in 1963.[22]

We would be remiss if we didn't share a unique positive experience for children and teens in the museum world.

- Museum of Jewish Heritage (NYC) exhibit: "Courage to Act: Rescue in Denmark"

An extraordinary exhibition for children aged 9 and up telling the remarkable story of the rescue of the Danish Jews during the Holocaust. Themes of separation, bravery and resilience inspire and engender empathy—an experience to share with the whole family.

Section III

Use Empathy, a Helpful Lens

We have a lot of work to do. All of us . . . from every background—every religion—living that value. Every life is sacred—every human is sacred.
—**Rabbi Charlie Cytron-Walker** (held hostage at Texas synagogue in 2021)

Do not judge your fellow until you have stood in his place.
—**Hillel,** *Pirkei Avot* 2:5

You've got to love Hillel, who was born around 110 BCE and was the first in recorded history to speak about "walking in others' shoes." That's empathy in a nutshell.

Here's another quote that encapsulates empathy. Julian Powe wrote in 2012 that "[e]mpathy helps us transform 'otherness' into inclusiveness." Researcher Simon Baron-Cohen [comedian Sacha's first cousin] defines empathy this way: "our ability to identify what someone else is thinking and feeling, and to respond to their thoughts and feelings with the appropriate emotion."[23]

Empathy creates better relationships, closer friendships, and stronger communities. It boosts children's social-emotional skills, strengthening them and their abilities to work and play with others.

Empathy is a cherished Jewish value because, with it, we and our children can:

- increase our understanding of "the others," those who differ from us in various ways by "walking in their shoes"

- broaden our perspective on the world and discover its varieties of living and enjoying

- explore fulfilling ways to show our concern and care for our diverse fellow beings.

A. Empathy—A Measured Decline for Youth

Recent research about empathy and youth is alarming. It tells us empathy is dropping, narcissism is increasing, and social-emotional skill development is being sacrificed for grades, testing and cell phones. Youth deficits for empathy, *rachmones* (Yiddish for mercy or compassion), and critical social-emotional skills are distressing. And COVID-19 has only made these skills worse.

B. Summoning Empathy for Self, the Jewish People, Israel, and Others

Empathy for Oneself—Self-Compassion

If you have experienced low self-esteem from time to time, you are not alone. Yet not a single benefit springs from being mired in the depths of despair for the "sin" of failing to be perfect. Parents overwhelmingly want to protect their sons and daughters from the angst of low self-esteem.

Self-compassion is a great treatment plan for low self-esteem. And you will not be surprised when we say the way to increase self-worth is ... yes, empathy! Before you extol empathy for others, be empathetic to yourself.

Kristen Neff, a professor of educational psychology at the University of Texas-Austin, defines self-compassion as "treating yourself with the same kindness and care you treat a friend," or stated more definitively, to be "kind and understanding toward one's self in instances of pain or failure rather than being harshly self-critical." Neff adds, "When we are self-compassionate, we remind ourselves: 'I am a human and the human condition is imperfect for all of us.'"[24]

Self-esteem is a judgment about how valuable you are, but self-compassion sidesteps this inner critical dialogue of woe. When children develop self-compassion, a burden is lifted from their shoulders. Self-compassion dovetails with Carol Dweck's "growth mind-set." Dweck, a renowned psychology researcher and professor from Stanford University, says, "One performs better out of a place of kindness for yourself than from a place of self-criticism and fear."[25]

Research indicates there are many benefits for those who practice self-compassion, including improving your mental health and the well-being of your family. Self-compassion is the foundation to build empathy for the Jewish people, Israel, and others.

Empathy for the Jewish People and Israel

> But above all, for Jews, what's changed is our place in the world—our sense of agency, self-reliance, and power. We've developed remarkable capacity and capability as a people.
> —**Doron Krakow,** President and CEO, JCC Association of North America

Fast-forwarding to today, we don't know all Jewish people and we don't know everyone in Israel, but we all know some Israeli people and perhaps have visited Israel.

For a minute, let's walk in the shoes of what it is like to be an Israeli citizen. Surrounded by Arab nations in the Middle East, Israel is the only democracy. Whether Baha'i, Arab, Muslim, Christian, or Ethiopian, secular or religious Jewish, most Israelis get along in this multicultural society. We just don't get to hear about it in the media.

In fact, what we love most about Israel is what you don't read in the news. There are about 150 interfaith, interreligious Israeli-Palestinian nonprofits or groups working together, such as Seeds for Peace and Rabbis for Human Rights. Sadly, the good news about people getting along does not merit "breaking news" status.

Untold News (untoldnews.org) is one of our favorite websites because it tells the positive parts of the story. Begun in 2010, it covers how Israel assists others with cutting-edge technology; medical, scientific, and environmental advances, and vital humanitarian work.

In addition to watching the videos, click the "Facebook/Untold News" heading to receive daily news. Another organization that has been offering unreported Israel news for 23 years is ISRAEL21C (israel21c.org). Check it out, too.

Please remember what we said earlier. Anti-Israel rhetoric is taking a toll on our college students across the United States, and they are unpracticed and unprepared.

* * *

There are ways of disagreeing with the policies of the Israeli government without sounding antisemitic. And blaming all Jews for something wrong that Israel has done—that's antisemitic.
—**Deborah E. Lipstadt**[26]

Empathy for Others

Diversity is not about how we differ.
Diversity is about embracing one another's uniqueness.
—**Ola Joseph, Nigerian-born speaker, author, consultant**

Those who do not grow, grow smaller.
—**Hillel, *Pirke Avot***

True empathy is for "the other"—the person we may never have met, may not be in our neighborhood, or worships another religion. True empathy is *tikkun olam* realized.

Tikkun olam extends to people we don't know well if at all, yet we can feel for them when we walk in their shoes. Often included in this group are people with disabilities, abused children, refugees, the homeless, and others outside the mainstream.

Starting in elementary school, children can understand empathy in a way they could not when they were preschoolers. Most six- or seven-year-olds are cognitively capable of walking in somebody else's shoes. They are ready to feel empathy and act on it in the form of sharing, supporting, and helping.

Middle school years are exciting and challenging. Preteens are becoming more independent and meeting new peers. Middle schoolers often are exploring their identity. They ask themselves questions such as "Who am I?" and "Who do I want to be?" Their answers influence the friendships they pursue. As a result, changes in friendships are common and sometimes difficult. In fact, as you probably know, middle school is when our kids are bullied, teased, and excluded the most.

Many middle schoolers seem to ignore adult advice and listen only to their peers. Yes, parents, we, too, know the all-too-familiar middle schooler grunt. We promise you: A human being is in there! In fact, with a bit of focused effort, conversation, and practice, adults—both parents and teachers—can increase children's empathy quotient to reduce exclusion, bullying, and cyberbullying.

Before leaving our discussion of middle school challenges, we must alert you to the pressure that awaits unsuspecting teens. Because antisemitism is a form of bullying, middle school is when antisemitism is the worst. What a great time for middle schoolers to learn and practice how to push back against antisemitic comments.

In high school, we still have the opportunity to improve empathy, empathic empowerment, and other social-emotional skills so our teens can learn to better respond to others and improve their life skills. Teens will abandon us soon for the "real world," so there's no time to lose.

C. Empathetic Action by UPstanders

> **Upstander:** A person who speaks or acts in support of an individual or cause, particularly someone who intervenes on behalf of a person being attacked or bullied.
> **—Oxford English Dictionary**

A most compelling and encouraging piece of research is that youth having a strong sense of identity—whether it be from religion, heritage, ethnicity, or country of origin—have the best psychological well-being and make the best UPstanders.[27] *Please read this sentence again slowly and let it really sink in.* Ergo, youth most secure in identity, are best capable of *standing up and speaking out.*

> Act the way you'd like to be and soon you'll be the way you act.
> **—Leonard Cohen, poet, singer**

We have shared how to focus on empathy for ourselves, the Jewish people, Israel, and others. Empathy is a good start, but empathy alone is not enough. As Jews, we need to take action. Empathy as a feeling is only a beginning. We need to transform empathy into empathetic action. We need to "stand up and speak out" and be an UPstander or a member of an UPstander team, group, or family.

> If I am not for myself, who will be for me? [empathy for self]
> If I am only for myself, then who am I? [empathy for others]
> And if not now, then when? [UPstanders taking action]
> **—Hillel, *Pirke Avot*, 1:14**

Most youth are reluctant to "stand up and speak out." We accept that few will even consider such action, but there are alternatives so that every Jewish young person can do something. Following are a few suggestions to prime the pump so you can think of other things your children can do:

- report antisemitism to an adult or organization (see Part Four)

- do research on bias and antisemitism and share what you've learned

- become a member of a team

- search for one Jewish person in your family/community who inspires you

Here's a woman who especially inspires us: Amid the transports from the Warsaw Ghetto to the death camps in the summer of 1942—and only half a year before she and her daughter Margalit were transported to Treblinka—artist Gela Seksztajn wrote her last will and testament:

"As I stand on the border between life and death, certain that I will not remain alive, I wish to take leave from my friends and my works . . . My works I bequeath to the Jewish Museum to be built after the war. Farewell, my friends. Farewell, the Jewish people. Never again allow such a catastrophe."

We were fortunate to see the will in the Ringelbaum archives, a collection of Jewish documents hidden and buried underground in steel cans and boxes during the Warsaw Ghetto uprising. Her testament to the last courageous resisters in the Warsaw Ghetto Uprising is a treasure.

Gela's words give us chills. There she is, sitting in the ghetto, knowing she will die, but also confident that future generations will hear her words. How does this make you feel? Take a moment. Then take a deep breath. Her words resonate much like the shofar's call on Rosh Hashanah:

The purpose of the shofar blast is to shake us up and to disturb our status quo. The shofar call *"shevarim"* literally means broken. And if you do not feel any cracks emerge from that sonic signal, you might ask yourself if you've truly fulfilled your obligation to hear it. For the shofar blast should be a wake-up call that reminds us to dig a little deeper, to bear into what is hard, to stop living life on the surface of it all.
—Rabbi Angela Buchdahl, Central Synagogue, New York City

Ethnic Identity + Religious Orientation = UPstanders

What is an UPstander? Empathic Action? And What Are Its Advantages?

Here is an UPstander story from Lynne:

> My son Jake (in high school at the time) was seated at a table in a pizza joint and overheard, "Hitler should have finished the job." He stood up, turned around to two men sitting at a table, and said: "Excuse me. I am Jewish and deeply offended by what you said."

They were flabbergasted, not realizing they were overheard. They backpedaled and said they didn't mean what they said. I was so, so proud of my son, an UPstander!
How do you construct an UPstander in a largely bystander society?

Don't worry if you don't know where to start. We are lucky that many psychologists were puzzled by this question and wanted to solve it. The mystery is unraveled by a Holocaust survivor in the 1930s named Sam who was curious.

In Poland, when Sam Oliner was twelve, the Nazis came to town and ordered his family to relocate to a Jewish ghetto. When the Nazis ordered his family onto the street, Samuel's stepmother yelled at him to run. Run he did, and eventually, he found a safe place at the home of a Catholic neighbor who knew his family before the war. At great peril to herself and her family, she took him in and hid him from the Gestapo. His life was saved. After the war, he emigrated to the United States and dedicated his life to understanding the altruism of people—to understand what motivated his neighbor to save him.

Oliner established the Altruistic Personality and Prosocial Behavior Institute at Humboldt State University in California. He interviewed and psychologically assessed more than seven hundred people who had risked their lives to rescue Jews in Nazi-occupied Europe. He found that "the rescuers were much more empathetic than the non-rescuers because they prized values of fairness, compassion and personal responsibility toward strangers." They had learned these values from their parents.[28]

Kristen Monroe, a professor at the University of California Irvine who has also researched the psychology of Holocaust rescuers, sums it up heartfully: "Where the rest of us see a stranger, an altruist sees a fellow human being."[29]

This research substantiates the importance of parents creating a home that values fairness, compassion, and caring about others.

> How wonderful it is that nobody needs to wait a single moment before starting to improve the world.
> —**Anne Frank**

Section IV

Be a T.E.A.M. with Your Child and Partner as a Family

A. The T.E.A.M. Approach

Parents and children together can advance to achieve success faster.

Give me a T, give me an E, give me an A, give me an M!

    T   **TOGETHER**

    E   **ELIMINATE**

    A   **ANTISEMITISM**

    M   **MOMENTUM** (the impetus gained by a moving object; strength that keeps growing)

Around the kitchen table or huddled together on a laptop, you and your family are compelled to act as a T.E.A.M., providing momentum through empathetic action. You are stronger together!

The Hebrew word for team is *k'votsa*. We created acronym initials for KVOTSA: *Kinder Vanting Optimistically to Stop Antisemitism* (please say this out loud with a Yiddish accent). Be creative and have some fun with this.

> Only the lesson which is enjoyed can be learned well.
> **—Talmud**

We share this inspirational quote because before you begin your interactive T.E.A.M. journey, we want you to know that education sticks when it is *fun*. Not every activity can be enjoyed, but please consider the Fun Factor. Your endeavor to create Jewish pride, empathy, and empowerment should be engaging, interactive, and include everyone in your home. Your T.E.A.M. could have grandparents, friends, and children's friends as members. We are a *shtetl* (community).

Variety is king in the Fun Factor realm. In addition to face-to-face discussion and sharing, consider adding other avenues of creative expression—art, videos, plays, music, poems, TikToks . . . you name it.

Recent research talks about the rising importance of belonging. Belonging and empathy are vital parts of relationships. Working together with each family member generates a sense of belonging not only to a *mishpacha* (family) but also to a community. It is important to belong and to feel included. Not belonging can lead to a dark place for children.

Steven Spielberg had been part of a deeply Jewish Orthodox experience in his early childhood, but when he got a little older, his family lived in places where they were the only Jews. He and his siblings became targets because they didn't belong. The antisemitism he faced led him to find the courage in adulthood to take a stand and make the Holocaust movie *Schindler's List*. The film not only became famous but creating it changed Spielberg's feelings toward his Jewish heritage:

> There was a lot of anti-Semitism against me and my sisters. In study hall kids used to pitch pennies at me, which would hit my desk and make a large clatter. It was called "pitching pennies at the Jew" and it was very hurtful. I got smacked and kicked to the ground during physical education. I was an Outsider, and as a result I wasn't proud of my Jewish heritage—I was ashamed. I was so ashamed of being a Jew but now I'm filled with pride.[30]

Occasionally, perhaps when a tragic antisemitic incident occurs, your T.E.A.M. may express the need to go beyond family discussions. That's a time to heed the advice of Fred Rogers, the host of the long-running television show "Mister Rogers Neighborhood." He reminded people to seek out the good—"the helpers"—when something bad happens. These helpers are people who come forward to assist. Your T.E.A.M. can reach out to helpers such as a rabbi, a medical professional who treats trauma, and organizations such as the ADL and AJC.

B. Tips—Not-So-Secret Boosters for Becoming an Effective T.E.A.M. Leader

We approach the T.E.A.M.-leader starting line with different strengths, motivations, and emotions to reduce antisemitism. The following tips can boost you to success regardless of your starting point. Just remember to do them!

Tip 1—Start with yourself! Your answers to the following questions are critical.

   a. So I can be thoroughly present, do I know and will I use techniques to calm myself before each T.E.A.M. meeting? (If your answer is no, for calming techniques, see PART TWO, Step Three, Activity: Calming.)

   b. Acknowledging that slow and steady makes learning easier, do I commit to aspire to a 15-to-20-minute T.E.A.M. meeting each week?

   c. Understanding that sometimes T.E.A.M. members need hours, days, or weeks to process information, can I avoid criticizing myself if the meeting does not go as I expected?

Tip 2—Schedule regular T.E.A.M. meetings. Make meetings a regular occurrence, not just when antisemitic incidents happen. Many activities in the guidebook can be accomplished during one meeting.

Tip 3—Use *only* active listening, which means hearing another's words with deliberate intention, by following these four key elements:

a. Pay face-to-face full attention to the speaker, making sure to avoid distractions, thoughts about your "to do" list, and sights and sounds in the environment.

b. Show that you are listening through open body language—nods, a smile, or short verbal comments such as "yes," "aha," "mmmm," or "that sounds interesting." Also, notice the speaker's body language.

c. Restate in your own words what the speakers said so they know if you understood their feelings and thoughts.

d. Defer judgment. Be empathetic, nonjudgmental, and consider what is said from the speaker's perspective.

Tip 4—Ask reflective questions. That means encouraging T.E.A.M. members to look back over what or how they have learned. The beauty of reflective questions is that they are open ended, so they can't be answered by "yes" or "no," and there is no right or wrong answer. The person answering is always the only authority!

a. Some strong reflective questions to use with the guidebook's activities are "What did I learn that I did not know before?" and "What are some ways I figured this out?" You can substitute "you" for "I" in the questions.

Tip 5—Respond with age appropriateness when discussing an antisemitic incident or tragedy.

a. Use a reassuring, positive voice and body language that gives the same message.

b. Invite the children/teens to share what happened or what they heard happened and their questions. If they offer incorrect or confusing information, respond, "That's so interesting. What makes you think that?" The answer will give you a hint of what information to provide.

c. Share only details about what the children/teens have expressed an interest in knowing, nothing more! Remember that the children/teens are the seekers, not you. Speak in vocabulary that the child can understand easily.

d. If the children/teens pose questions to which you have no answer, be honest and respond that you don't know. You might suggest researching and finding the answer together.

Part Two

Upstander Activities

Responding to antisemitism is a skill that improves with practice. You are entering the Activity Zone, where you will get that practice. You don't have to do all the activities. Do the ones that speak to you and your family. You might start by reviewing them yourself or jumping in together with a child, tween, or teen, or the whole family. Give everyone paper, (or maybe a T.E.A.M. journal), compare notes, and discuss. True learning takes place during the face-to-face discussions.

If you are not somewhat familiar with the width and breadth of antisemitism, which has haunted us for millennia, please spend some time on books, videos, webinars, and other programs to educate yourself.

We are inspired by Elie Wiesel:

> Silence encourages the tormentor, never the tormented. Sometimes we must interfere.
> —**Elie Wiesel,** Holocaust survivor and winner of Nobel Peace Prize

The purpose of this section's activities is threefold: 1) to establish pride and strengthen identity for Jewish youth; 2) to create empathy for self, the Jewish people, Israel, and others; and 3) to encourage Jewish parents to foster Jewish youth UPstanders—those trained and practiced to "stand up and speak out" against antisemitism and bias and seek help when safety issues arise.

Please note: The main thing is to practice. Responding to antisemitism is a skill that improves with practice. The benefits of practice are higher quotients of preparedness, perseverance, mastery, and confidence.

With your family T.E.A.M., get ready to take three bold steps into your Jewish heritage journey. You can do the steps in order or pick and choose how you go about them. Whatever you decide, concentrate on having fun and embracing Judaism's gifts.

> Our goal should be to live life in radical amazement . . . get up in the morning and look at the world in a way that takes nothing for granted. Everything is phenomenal, everything is incredible; never treat life casually. To be spiritual is to be amazed.
> **—Rabbi Abraham Joshua Heschel**

Step One

Building Jewish Identity and Pride

> He who does not increase knowledge, decreases it.
> —Hillel, *Pirke Avot*

Consider accepting the responsibility of increasing Jewish knowledge and pride before your children graduate from high school.

ACTIVITY: How Does This Make You Feel?

- reading a Jewish author

- seeing a Jewish person in the media

- hearing that Israel is helping other countries

- hearing that Israel shares its technology with the world

- celebrating Hanukkah or Passover

- lighting Sabbath candles

ACTIVITY: Encountering Antisemitism

ENCOUNTERING ANTISEMITISM

	HOW DOES THIS MAKE YOU FEEL?	DID YOU TAKE ACTION?
Seeing antisemitism online example: cyberbullying		
Feeling powerless and not knowing what to do in face of antisemitism and other bias		
Overhearing an antisemitic remark		
Hearing 'dirty Jew,' 'Jew bastard,' or 'Christ killer'		
Hearing 'Jew'em Down'		
When you hear a Jewish stereotype		
Hearing a Muslim or Asian stereotype		
Hearing Israel is an Apartheid state		
Hearing that Israel hates Palestinians		

ACTIVITY: Your Jewish Favorites

- favorite Jewish moment

- favorite Jewish song

- favorite Jewish food

- funniest Jewish moment

- saddest Jewish moment

ACTIVITY: A Bit of History

Directions: For each date, tell how old you were.

- **August 2017**: At the white supremacist protest against the removal of Confederate monuments in Charlottesville, Virginia, crowds chanted loudly and repeatedly, "You will not replace us. Jews will not replace us."

- **March 2019**: Fifty-nine graves at the Hebrew Cemetery in Falls River, Massachusetts, were vandalized with swastikas and antisemitic slurs written in black marker. Messages included Hitler statements, such as "Expel the Jews."

- **April 2019**: On the last day of Passover, which fell on Shabbat, a man entered the Chabad of Poway (California) synagogue. Using a semiautomatic rifle, he killed a worshiper. Earlier that day, he had posted an open letter online stating that the Jews were preparing a meticulously planned genocide of the European race.

- **December 2019**: At Pittsburgh's Tree of Life Synagogue during Shabbat morning services, a man with a gun entered and killed eleven people who were praying.

- **January 2022**: During Shabbat morning prayers, the rabbi and three members at Congregation Beth Israel in Colleyville, Texas, were held hostage for eleven hours by an armed man demanding the release of a Pakistani national serving a prison sentence in Texas.

Think About:

- In what ways are these Bits of History alike?

- In what ways are these Bits of History different?

- Did having to write how old you were for each Bit of History influence your thinking?

- If you answered no, why not? If you answered yes, how?

ACTIVITY: One Person *Can* Make a Difference.

For Jewish youth to "stand up and speak out" against bias and stereotypes, they need to believe that action is possible and worth the effort. They need to believe that one person can make a difference. So, let's inspire them with a litany of Jewish heroes—starting in Biblical times to today.

Here's a brief list. Can you add some? Other than being a celebrity, how did they give back?

Today's Jewish Celebrities that give back:
1. **Debra Messing:** She has put her Jewish identity front and center in speaking out against antisemitism and other injustices.

2. **Juju Chang:** The Korean American of ABC's *Nightline* converted to Judaism.

3. **Gal Gadot:** The Israeli actor gives back. Search online to find out how.

4. **Alana Haim:** She stars in the movie "Licorice Pizza." The three Haim sisters and their parents put on charity concerts.

5. **Natalie Portman:** The actor, who was born in Israel, helped launch an international campaign to bring financial services to one million of the world's lowest income families through one hundred thousand "Village Banks." She supports more than twenty other charities, including lowland gorillas in Africa.

6. **Leonard Cohen:** The singer, poet, songwriter, novelist, and musician gave us the song "Hallelujah" and many others.

7. **Adam Sandler and Jerry Seinfeld:** These comedians support many charities.

8. **Idina Menzel:** The singer/actor and **Taye Diggs** created a foundation to help girls from urban communities.

9. **Barbra Streisand:** Did you know she has a foundation? Research and share.

10. **Paul Newman:** Profits from the late actor's food products go to a foundation. Of blessed memory and blue eyes' gorgeousness, find out where the donations go.

11.   Here are more celebrities for you to check out: **Michael Douglas, Dustin Hoffman, Jack Klugman, Daveed Diggs,** and **Rashida Jones.**

ACTIVITY: Famous Groundbreaking Jewish Heroes

We suggest researching together as a family or separately and then sharing. Here are some heroes from various categories: Hank Greenberg, former U.S. Senator Joe Lieberman, Eddie Cantor, Leonard Bernstein, and Golda Meir.

- **Sports**: Yeshiva University College basketball (longest winning streak in men's college basketball) and Sandy Koufax

- **Science**: Albert Einstein and Lise Meitner

- **Helping refugees**: Hannah Senesh

- **Poets and writers**: Emma Lazarus, J. D. Salinger, Franz Kafka and Lillian Hellman

- **Cartoonist**: Rube Goldberg

- **Government**: Menachem Begin, Golda Meir and Raphael Lemkin

- **Civil rights:** Rabbi Abraham Joshua Heschel

- **Military**: Capt. Alfred Dreyfus (the Dreyfus Affair) and Yonathan Netanyahu

ACTIVITY: RBG

Here's another person who inspires us—the late Supreme Court Justice Ruth Bader Ginsberg. If you haven't seen the movie *On the Basis of Sex* (about fighting for gender equality) or seen the museum exhibit "Notorious RBG," we urge you to do so with your family.

Ginsburg took hope one step further when she said, "Fight for the things that you care about, but do it in a way that will lead others to join you."

How much more can we accomplish when we align with our family and others to accomplish social justice for Jews and others?

ACTIVITY: Jewish Partisans and Righteous Gentiles

- Do you know these Holocaust resisters and partisans from the Holocaust: Frank Blaichman, and Gertrude Boyarski (hint: check out jewishpartisans. org)

- Look up these Righteous Among the Nations: Jan Karski, Oscar Schindler, and Aristides de Sousa Mendes

- What is a "Righteous" Gentile?

- How many Jewish partisans fought in World War II? What percentage of these partisans were women?

ACTIVITY: Can You Share Some of Your Favorite Jewish Heroes That We Haven't Mentioned?

If you cannot recollect any, do some research online or in books with your family. Or you can suggest researching a Jewish person you admire.

> If we don't respect those who came before us, and who made our existence possible, how can we expect anyone to respect us?
> —**Professor Barry Rubin, author of *Children of Dolhinov: Our Ancestors and Ourselves***

ACTIVITY: Relatives Are a Source of Pride

A frequently overlooked treasure in building Jewish pride is the simple action of asking older relatives—such as aunts, uncles, and grandparents—to talk about their childhoods and adult lives. Here's one story about Harlene's great-grandfather, her very first family member to become a citizen of the United States.

My great-grandfather was a pioneer and adventurer. He came by himself to America right after the Civil War and settled in Nashville, Tennessee. In those days, the only thing a Jewish immigrant could do was peddle with his pack on his back. Eventually, he saved enough money to buy a horse and a wagon. After two years of working, he had accumulated sufficient funds, so he sent for my great-grandmother and their children, who had remained in the old country. What persistence, ingenuity, and love of family!

Pique your children's curiosity and interview grandparents and other older family members.

ACTIVITY: A Jewish Identity Memory Box for the Family or Individuals

Put in your favorites—a Jewish recipe, mezuzah, poem, memory, prayer, recording of your grandparents, drawing, and so on. Then put it away for a while to discover later.

> When we give children clear and consistent messages about what is more important [through what we say and what we do], they are more likely to be inspired to act on those values—and to become adults who draw on the rich and enduring principles of Judaism to build a meaningful and fulfilling life.
> —**Maurice Elias, author, *The Joys and Oys of Parenting***

ACTIVITY: We Are Only 0.2 Percent of the Population

As a Jewish people, we are only 0.2 percent of the world's population, yet we endure bias and hate extremely disproportionate to our numbers. We have endured antisemitism for centuries. Answer this: Why is that?

ACTIVITY: If You Do Only One Thing

If you do only one thing to build identity and pride every day, what would it be?

Examples: saying the *b'racha* (blessing) for one meal each day, saying the Shema each night before you go to bed, kissing the mezuzah or wearing a Jewish star or *kippah* (skullcap)

Brainstorm some examples that fit you and your family.[31]

ACTIVITY: I Spy Empathy, Kindness, Compassion

Think about the last few days. Did you or your children observe a person, animal, or something in nature that depicted any of these positive behaviors?

Briefly describe your observation. Then ask, "What did I spy: empathy, kindness, compassion? Have other participants answer.

Step Two

Fostering Empathy for Oneself, Jewish People, Israel, and Others

ACTIVITY: Jewish Values

We shared our Jewish values in the first section. Answer the following questions:

1. What are your family values?

2. What are the values of every member of your family?

3. What are your grandparents' values? Are yours the same or different? Why?

ACTIVITY: Quotes to Discuss in Your Home—What Do They Mean?

Quotes by Jews are provided below. Discuss them and answer the following questions, and make sure to truly listen to each other:

1. What does this quote say to you?

2. How does the fact that the words are stated by a Jew make you feel?

3. Does this quote inspire you to action? How? Why?

Give me your tired, your poor,
Your huddled masses yearning to breathe free,
The wretched refuse of your teeming shore.
Send these, the homeless, tempest-tossed, to me:
I lift my lamp beside the golden door.
—**Emma Lazarus,** inscribed on plaque at bottom of Statue of Liberty

The opposite of love is not hate, it's indifference. The opposite of art is not ugliness, it's indifference. The opposite of faith is not heresy, it's indifference. And the opposite of life is not death, it's indifference.
—**Elie Wiesel**

[The Jew] is a born rebel … endowed with a shrewd, logical mind, in order that he may examine and protest; with a stout and fervent heart in order that the instinct of liberty may grow into a consuming passion . . .
—**Emma Lazarus**—An Epistle to the Hebrews

No one has ever become poor by giving.
—**Anne Frank**

She was the toughest, wisest person I ever knew. My daughter always fought for what was right. My daughter despised bullies and would put herself in the middle of someone being bullied to make it stop.
—**Fred Guttenberg** reflecting on his daughter, Jaime, age 14, who sadly was murdered by a mass shooter in Parkland, Florida, in 2018; we include her to inspire other Jewish youth Upstanders.

We cannot change the past, but the survivors have shown us that out of the wreckage of destruction, something can be redeemed from the past, if we fight hate with love, brutality with compassion, and death with an unconquerable dedication to life.
—**Rabbi Jonathan Sacks**

I want to be a Jewish hero to kids who are going to look up to me and show them that you can stay true to your religion, stay true to your convictions, and still fulfill all your potential in life, including athletically.
—**Ryan Turell,** 2021 college basketball leading scorer, 2022, NCAA Division III National Player of the Year

This needs a bigger spotlight. This should be a national scandal. We need action rather than words. I call on all people, the media, and politicians from every side to stand with us and be louder against antisemitism. Enough is enough.
—**British TV personality Rachel Riley** speech to British Parliament, March 2022

ACTIVITY: Develop Empathy for and Honor Jewish Ancestors
If our courageous ancestors didn't escape Europe, we would not be here. We owe them our very lives.

Genealogy activities can be designed to encourage local Jewish youth to bring the history of Jewish life alive by creating living memorials for those buried in our cemeteries. Students can honor our Jewish ancestors, including those who left their homes to escape persecution, pogroms, and poverty in search of a better life by telling their stories.

In addition to family trees, youth can make posters, interview grandparents and great-grandparents, make a TikTok, write a poem, reenact the story of their immigrant passage from Europe, etc. Please visit gtjcp.org to see how we are creating youth reenactors.

ACTIVITY: AJC Translate Hate Quiz
This is fascinating to do by yourself or with family members. Take it together with a tween or teen. It helps us understand what we do and don't know about antisemitism.

Visit https://www.ajc.org/translatehatequiz.

ADL QUIZ. Visit jewishupstanders.org for the link

The Holocaust

ACTIVITY: Make the Holocaust Personal
Lynne shares the following:

> My Jewish ancestors were murdered in Ukraine, Poland, Ukraine, and Latvia. If my grandparents and great-grandparents didn't come to the U.S., I would not be here. If your ancestors didn't make their way to the U.S., Israel, South Africa, Cuba, Uruguay, China, Japan or Argentina, they were murdered.
>
> Harlene and I just listened to a webinar about Jews who fled Germany and bravely traveled through China to Japan. Wow, that survival story is something to research.
>
> Lynne's grandfather Louis, from Belarus, tried to save his sisters and brothers, but his letters to the U.S. embassy pleading for help were to no avail. It's heartbreaking. They were all murdered.
>
> Our Jewish kids don't realize they are the lucky ones. If your ancestors did not leave Europe, your family would not exist. Let's walk in the shoes of our ancestors, leaving their families and homes, not speaking English, with little money in their pockets, alone on a steamship, never to see their families again. These discussions might pique interest in heritage, genealogy, and honoring those who came before us or died in the Holocaust.

ACTIVITY: Commemorate the Holocaust in Your Home in a Personal Way

- Brainstorm with your family.

- Tell stories.

- Light a candle.

- Read poetry or stories together—every member brings something to share.

- Cite a prayer.

- Sing Jewish songs of pride.

- Talk about Jewish partisans or Righteous Among the Nations.

- Watch Holocaust movies—and discuss (as appropriate developmentally).

- Take your family to listen to a survivor in person or via a webinar.

- Celebrate Yom HaShoah.

Israel

Israel is a democracy and welcomes Jews and peoples of different religions from all over the world. No democracy is perfect, including our own in the United States.

ACTIVITY: Israel Defense Forces (IDF)

The IDF defends Israel and helps people around the world. The IDF assists during hurricanes, earthquakes, and disasters.

Discuss why Israel's aid to other countries is rarely in the news. As we write this, Israel is accepting thousands of refugees from Ukraine—both Jewish and non-Jewish.

ACTIVITY: What Does Your Family Know about Israel?

- What do you know about Israel?

- What do you appreciate about Israel?

ACTIVITY: Visit Israel (in Person or Virtually)

Israel is fabulous for many things:

- Multifaith—Muslim, Christian, and Greek Orthodox

- History

- Archeology—Roman, Greek, Bedouin, Bronze, and Iron Age

- Geology

- Food

- Music and dance

- Museums, especially Yad Vashem in Jerusalem and modern art

If you don't have the resources to visit, consider a virtual trip for the whole family—offered frequently by the Jewish National Fund.

ACTIVITY: Giving Back by Traveling to Israel and Volunteering

Consider participating in Volunteers for Israel and traveling there with your family or a friend to help out in real time. Sure, you can travel and have fun, but consider giving back during your vacation, too. Please visit https://vfi-usa.org/.

ACTIVITY: The United Nations

We could write a whole book about this one. Please educate yourself. The State of Israel suffers a long history of bias and discrimination at the hands of the United Nations. As the only democracy in the Middle East, Israel is picked on. The ADL and AJC's magazine *Commentary* are good sources on the topic. Search antisemitism and the United Nations to learn more.

ACTIVITY: Connect Your Child to The Community

Take your children to antisemitism and pro-Israel rallies and marches.

Step Three

Creating and Becoming Jewish Youth UPstanders

The Jewel in the Crown

Esther's Crown

We all know the story of Queen Esther and how she stood up and saved her Jewish people. She was one of the earliest Jewish UPstanders, an inspiration through her heroism. We remind parents and teachers that only by providing youth frequent opportunities to practice UPstander activities will they be able to act successfully in antisemitic, biased and bullying situations. To create Upstanders i.e. those who can "stand up and speak out," it is critical that you practice these skills regularly.

ACTIVITY: Acts of Lovingkindness

The Hebrew term *g'muilut chasadim* means bestowing "acts of lovingkindness." The concept encompasses giving *tzedakah* (charity), welcoming guests, visiting the sick, and giving of ourselves to help others. In fact, Jewish tradition tells us that performing acts of loving-kindness is even more important than giving money to tzedakah.[32]

- What do you do to help others?
- What does your family do to help others?
- What does your synagogue do?
- Research and discuss.

ACTIVITY: A Precious Gift—Bubbe and Zayde

Most kids have an affinity for their grandparents and will take suggestions from them, modeling their behavior, and so on.

- What do or did your grandparents do to help others? when your parents were children?

- After your parents were living on their own? For your parents now?

ACTIVITY: Encountering Antisemitism

Remember this activity from Part One? After learning about empathic action (as UPstanders), what might you do differently?

ENCOUNTERING ANTISEMITISM
Remember this activity from Part I...after learning about UPstanders, what might you do differently?

	WHAT MIGHT YOU DO DIFFERENTLY NEXT TIME?	DID YOU PRACTICE?
Seeing antisemitism online example: cyberbullying		
Feeling powerless and not knowing what to do in face of antisemitism and other bias		
Overhearing an antisemitic remark		
Hearing 'dirty Jew,' 'Jew bastard,' or 'Christ killer'		
Hearing 'Jew'em Down'		
When you hear a Jewish stereotype		
Hearing a Muslim or Asian stereotype		
Hearing Israel is an Apartheid state		
Hearing that Israel hates Palestinians		

Famous composer Leonard Bernstein urges us on with this quote: "Stillness is our most intense mode of action. It is in our moments of deep quiet that is born every idea, emotion, and drive which we eventually honor with the name of action."

Theodor Herzl

Herzl dreamed of a Jewish homeland. His dream came true for all of us, reminding us that one person can make a huge difference.

ACTIVITY: What Is Your Dream?

Discuss what your dream is for yourself and each member of your family.

ACTIVITY: Reading Together to Process Empathy and Action

Intuitively, we know how to read to our kids, but there is an extra step you might be missing. Processing for learning! Discussing stories and facts enables processing—this is how kids learn. Although we know reading and *walking in the shoes* of books' characters creates empathy, discussing and using prompts might go beyond and create empathic action.

Discussion prompts:
1. How was that character feeling?

2. What would you have done in that situation?

3. How might you prepare for the next bias or antisemitic incident?

ACTIVITY: Sharing Your History Encountering Antisemitism

We suspect most parents and grandparents don't share their incidents of encountering antisemitism. We recommend that you take a few moments and write yours down. Confer with your spouse or significant other and discuss first. Schedule a meeting to share what is developmentally appropriate for the child's age.

Why? Research supports that knowing that their own family has suffered the shame, trauma, and embarrassment of being "the other" enables children to feel less alone and isolated.

ACTIVITY: Be a Mensch and Use Your Yiddish

Aren't we lucky to have Yiddish when English fails? Yiddish often has a great word to articulate emotion and humor. Like *mispacha, oy vey, schmendrick, schlemazel, schlemiel, kvelling, rachmones* and so on.

ACTIVITY: Tzedakah Box

Do you have a tzedakah box in your house? If not, have fun and make one together and watch all the extra change build up.

Then have a meeting to choose the charities to which your children want to donate. If there's a lull, share what you are passionate about and the organizations that support this.

ACTIVITY: Teach with Documentaries and Movies

Use documentaries and movies to discuss Jewish pride and/or UPstanderness with your family. Movies can foster social-emotional learning, creativity, and motivation.

Harlene's and Lynne's favorites

Harlene and Lynne prefer movies about Jewish partisans, Anne Frank, and Righteous Among the Nations. Here are some others:

- *Jojo's Rabbit*

- *The Pianist*

- *Fiddler on the Roof*—Who was better? Topol or Zero Mostel?

- *Yentl*

- *The Book Thief*

- *Exodus* starring Paul Newman

- *The Band's Visit*

- *The Garden of Finzi Continis*—When the fascists become stronger, they crash the shielded world of European Jews who'd been sheltered from growing antisemitism- because of their wealth.

Discussion prompts—Who took UPstander or empathic action? Who did not? Why?

ACTIVITY: Taking a Jewish Journey with a Journal or Diary

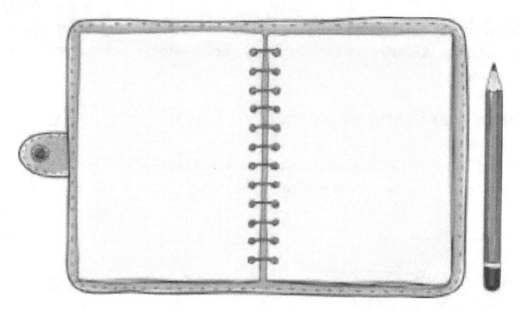

Here are questions to keep in mind as you go on a Jewish journey:

- What I learned today in our Jewish UPstander discussion

- Questions I have

- What I need help with

After you sort through the activities and resources, you might want to explore further by researching topics together. For example, AJC has a comprehensive glossary of tropes and memes and there are a multitude of websites that explore Jewish partisans during World War II. Sit down together at the computer or with a tablet and explore some of the information together. A team approach will strengthen all of you.

ACTIVITY: Stereotypes Used in Your Family

As Jews, we need to be aware of the danger of stereotypes that are harmful and create bias and discrimination.

What stereotypes do you and your family use? Examples: all Mexicans like tacos, or all Black persons have rhythm.

Have a family discussion about the slippery slope of stereotypes.

ACTIVITY: Afraid to Ask for Help

You Don't Have to Solve Conflicts Alone

At Kidsbridge, we have learned that kids are oftentimes afraid to ask for help from adults *and* peers. One of the reasons is that they are unpracticed.
Have your child practice asking for an adult's help using one of the following scenarios:

    a. being called a name

    b. being excluded

    c. hearing a stereotype

    d. seeing a peer threaten to harm themselves

    e. hearing bias or hate against a peer

Wouldn't you love to hear this from your son or daughter after a little practice dealing with antisemitism?

> Before I spoke out about antisemitism, I was afraid, believing that I would offend someone if I shared my feelings. But then I realized that biased statements and willful blindness create and sustain bigotry, thereby harming people and undermining our communities. I realized that if even just one other person listened and joined the fight, my voice would be doubled. Together, the louder our battle cry will be.
> —**Everett Rattray,** high school senior[33]
> Are you *kvelling* yet?

ACTIVITY: Calming

In the Kidsbridge Youth Center, we use an evidence-based system of strategies, meaning they are tried and true. After students practice for four hours in the Kidsbridge Center or for four one-hour sessions in their own classroom, they are better prepared for the next name-calling, bullying, or bias incident. Not only are they mentally ready and in an anticipatory state, but they also have a choice of several different strategies. Regardless of their age, before we introduce any strategy, we model, teach, and practice different calming techniques with the students. Calming one's mind and body is the first crucial step to success with any strategy!

Deep breathing or belly breaths are the foundation of most calming techniques. Follow the directions below, practice by yourself, and then model and teach them to your children:

With palms open, put one hand on or near your belly button. Put the other hand on top of that hand. If comfortable, close your eyes. Otherwise, fix your eyes on an unmoving object in front of you or on the floor.

Breathe in deeply. Feel your hands move up. Hold your breath as you silently count to three.

Exhale gently, pretending to blow out a birthday candle. Feel your hands move down. Repeat all steps.

Here are three different calming techniques. Try them all to discover which you like. Some of them you can do without anyone being aware that you are calming.

Shape Breathing:

a. Choose a shape—triangle, square, rectangle, heart, and so on. Choose where you want to finger-draw the shape: inside of your arm, cheek, upper thigh, or another spot.

b. With the index finger of one hand, draw one side of the shape while belly breathing. Keep the other palm on or near your belly button.

c. Hold your breath as you silently count to three.

d. With your index finger, draw another side of your shape while you exhale.

e. Repeat all steps three to five times until you feel your mind and body relax and you are calm.

Finger Breathing

   a. Hold one hand in front of your belly, with thumb and fingers spread widely apart.

   b. With the index finger of your other hand, slide up the outer side of your thumb as you belly breathe.

   c. Hold your breath as you silently count to three.

   d. Slide the index finger down the opposite side of your thumb as you breathe out gently.

   e. Repeat these steps for each of the four fingers until you feel your mind and body relax and you are calm.

Star of David Breathing

   a. Figure 2.7 shows the Star of David technique. Using belly breaths, follow the written directions on the drawing to calm yourself and others in your family.

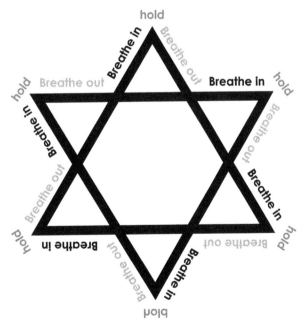

ACTIVITY: UPstander Strategies to Teach Your Children

We are indebted to Stan Davis, learned guru of research for bullying prevention and name-calling strategies. In Resources, you will see the useful books he has written.

Davis has worked as a child and family therapist in residential treatment, community mental health, and private practice. He became a school guidance counselor in the mid-1980s and began to focus on bullying prevention in the late 1990s. Davis trained educators, parents, and students nationwide in effective bullying prevention. He is a certified bullying prevention consultant and a founding member of the International Bullying Prevention Association.

As a research scholar surveying more than 10,000 youth, he is the gold standard in youth strategies and best practices. We've modified these strategies and teach them to youth in the Kidsbridge Center and outreach programs on how to respond to bullying, exclusion, bias and name-calling.

Be aware that the following strategies are also effective if your children or teens are being bullied in class in any situation involving name-calling or negative comments of any type—not just antisemitic.

Assertive behavior and strategies

Building on Stan's strategies, we added some new ones and reclassified them. Youths' success with immediate, right after and later strategies depends on their consistent use of three key assertive behaviors. Why? The way we hold our bodies and show expressions on our faces can reinforce the words we say, but often our body language speaks louder than our words. Passive and aggressive behaviors do not produce the results we want, but assertive behaviors do.

Regardless of the strategy, children and teens need to practice the three key assertive behaviors so that they always do them when delivering any strategy:

- **Sit or stand with a balance of strength and relaxation.**
- **Look at the person with direct eye contact and a calm expression on your face.**
- **Speak clearly, confidently, and respectfully.**

Some youth find that self-reminding by silently expressing, "I can be assertive." before beginning an immediate, right after or later strategy gives them the courage to act. Assertive behaviors not only reassure the target person, but also inform the oppressor of the responder's strength.

Safety Note: Assertive behavior is best *unless* there is a safety issue where harm is a possibility.

Immediate Strategies

Choose one of the following strategies to do *immediately* when an antisemitic remark is made to you or someone for whom you want to be an UPstander:

These strategies are coded to be developmentally appropriate. Some strategies will work for middle and high school, but not for elementary youth. That said, there are always exceptions to the rule, and you know your child best.

Key:

Elementary youth E

Middle schoolers M

High schoolers H

College C

1. **Walk away** yourself, or walk the person away. If you do not feel physically or emotionally safe, remember you are allowed to advocate for yourself and a fellow Jew by leaving the conversation. If you feel physically and psychologically safe, you can say something. (More about what you might say under "Have a private talk.") (E, M, H, C)

2. **Create a distraction**: Draw attention to something else that is happening nearby. Some call this interruption. (E, M, H, C)

Right After Strategy

Let a trusted adult know. (E, M, H, C)
How do you know trusted adults? They listen to you without interrupting, accept your view of the problem, suggest "doable" solutions and are o. k. with waiting until YOU are ready to take action.

Choose your trusted adults:

- Parents, Step-parents, Guardian

- Relatives—Grandfather, Grandmother, brother, Sister, Aunt, Uncle, Cousin

- Jewish Community—Rabbi, Cantor, Religious School Teacher, Youth Group Leader

- School—Teacher, Advisor/Counselor, Principal, Assistant Principal

- Others - ?

My trusted adults are:

Sometimes you are not comfortable in talking to a trusted adult by yourself so you want to take a supportive friend or two with you. Whom would you ask to go along?

Important Safety Note: In bullying situations that include a safety issue such as a threat of physical violence, one crucial step is mandatory. "Let a trusted adult know" must be done right after your child finishes doing one of the immediate strategies.

Later Strategies

Choose one of the following strategies to do *later,* depending on the situation.

1. **Cheer the target up**. Remember the target may be someone else or yourself. (E, M, H, C) Sometimes the most powerful thing we can do is call someone and listen to them.

2. **Make a plan for next time**. There is nothing wrong with delaying; we all benefit from 20/20 hindsight. No one is perfect. (E, M, H, C)

3. **Have a talk with the target.** (M, H, C)
   In a private situation, talk with the target. The target is feeling isolated, alone, and helpless. Actively listening to targets decreases their loneliness and vulnerability.

4. **Have a talk with the offender.** (mature M, H, C)
   In a private situation, follow the talk with offenders tips.

Talk with Offenders Tips

1. You have three choices when you observe someone committing an antisemitic microaggression (a verbal, behavioral, or environmental action that communicates negative, derogatory, or hostile slights and/or insults to the target person or group):

   a. Let it go.

   b. Respond immediately and have a talk with the offender.

   c. Respond later and have a talk with the offender.

2. Before choosing from the three options, consider your association with the person who made the remark. If you have a friendly relationship with the speaker and want to keep the friendship, you may feel more comfortable with responding either immediately or later (see below). If you have no relationship, responding will take more courage.

What follows are guidelines if you choose to respond immediately or respond later:

3. Make sure that you calm yourself before you respond. Use whatever calming technique works for you, such as:

    a. deep (belly) breathing

    b. shape breathing

    c. muscle tensing/relaxing, progressive muscle relaxation

    d. yoga

4. Before you respond, in your mind and emotions, separate the hurt from the impact of what was said or done (it might have been said without malicious intent). Be sure to give the offender the benefit of the doubt.

5. Monitor yourself to talk about what the individual did. Never talk about what the individual *is*—in other words, labeling the person.

    Example: A classmate who is a friend of yours shows you a bracelet. They comment: "It's just what I wanted and I *jewed* the owner down to half of the price he initially asked."

6. *Do* say in a conversational tone, "Help me understand what you mean by: 'I *jewed* the owner down'"? (You mention only what the individual *did* by repeating the words she said.) *Do not* say, "You are an antisemitic person." (Labeling a person may make the situation worse because it angers the recipient; they don't perceive their bias.)

7. Steady yourself. Being an UPstander is challenging work, requiring courage and determination. Resolve to be completely willing to hear the other person's perspective. Control your reaction to what the person shares; often you will experience a rise in your anger, aggravation, or frustration about the person's ignorance. Focus on having a conversation. Come from a place of curiosity, not blame.

8. Always invite the individual to sit or stand beside you, better than across from you. Being alongside one another is more conducive to solving the problem together while facing each other is more confrontational. State that the conversation may become uncomfortable.

9. The following are common reactions to immediate and later responses and UPstanders' next steps:

   a. Asking for clarification gives them a chance to check themselves. They will often say they did not know what they said or did was offensive.

   b. Verbalize that you accept what they said about their intentions. Then clearly explain how you initially interpreted what they did and why it impacted you. Focus on their doing or saying something inappropriate or making a mistake. Avoid making the individual into a bad person.

   c. Frequently, the person persists in asserting they didn't mean any harm. End the conversation by reminding them that you value their willingness to clarify their intent and hope that they appreciate your willingness to clarify their impact.

10. Here are some conversation openers for UPstanders:

   a. Help me understand what you mean by (insert words used or action done),

   b. I can see how you might think that, but I'm not sure if you're aware that this is how I'm receiving what was said (or done). Was that your intention?

   c. That made me feel uncomfortable.

   d. Tell me more.

   e. I am really curious and want to understand why you said (or did) that.

   f. Hold on. I need a minute to process what you just said (or did).

   g. Help me understand your thinking.

ACTIVITY: Practice, Practice, Practice

In the Kidsbridge Youth Center, Harlene and Lynne inform visiting students that bias and name-calling are going to happen to them or their friends tomorrow, next week, next month, or next year—even if they have been lucky enough to escape it until now. These instances are coming and we all need to anticipate them. Preparing is easy when you practice. We use skits and scenarios, and the students figure out solutions and act them out. We invite you and your family to practice skits and scenarios … and have fun doing it.

The best practice is to follow up by obtaining feedback involving the youth and the parent focusing on and talking about the specifics of effective action and positive results *or* the ineffective solution and how to modify that. Then the parent reteaches the technique and practice begins again.

Practice, Feedback, Reteach, Practic

Practice: Select an Upstander strategy you think would resonate with your child or family.

Feedback: Obtain feedback after the child has a chance to perform the strategy they have practiced. The child rates whether the strategy worked (fine, pretty good, or not so good).

Reteach (Note: Skip this step if the feedback answer is "fine."): Analyze the feedback and figure out any mistakes made by the child or problems in the situation that were not caused by them. Decide how to correct the mistakes or problems when the strategy is performed again. Model the steps in the Upstander strategy, one at a time, making sure to accentuate any changes the child will need to be successful.

Practice: Practice the "reteach" version of the activity with the child a minimum of three times or until they are comfortable leading. Caution: If after a half dozen practices the child still is unsuccessful, advise them that another activity is a better choice and teach that strategy instead.

> You might worry that the solutions you have generated—such as helping targets get away from bullying, telling an adult, or sitting with a lonely peer at lunch— might not make a difference. Gandhi acknowledged this fear when he said, "Whatever you do will be insignificant. But it is very important that you do it."[34]
> **—Stan Davis**

Tips for Elementary UPstanders' Techniques

1. **The Strategies:** Some elementary students will not be developmentally advanced enough to implement "Have a talk with the target" strategy. Parental guidance will be needed to help these elementary-age students build and repeatedly practice two powerful skills—assertiveness and calming—so they can successfully use the other strategies against antisemitism for themselves or another. Just a reminder that those five strategies are: create a distraction (interrupt), walk yourself or the other person away, let a trusted adult know, cheer yourself or the other person up, and make a plan for the next time.

   Note: If your children are very hesitant in coping with difficult situations, you need to also spend time helping build their friendship-making and social skills. First, strengthen their ability to begin and maintain a conversation. Once your children succeed in simply saying "Hi" to others, model asking questions and have them practice questioning, which is one of the easiest ways to keep a conversation going. Remind your children to ask for help if they feel unsure or uncomfortable. Asking shows you are intelligent.

2. **Calming:** Remind your child that if they or a friend is on the receiving end of hurtful words or actions, they have every right to feel and be angry. However, to take control and get back power, they must calm down. Of the various calming techniques (belly breathing, shape breathing, finger breathing, and tracing Star of David), your child will find one or more favorites.

If your children don't find any of these effective enough, try:

- Palm-pressing: Sit up straight. Open both hands with palms facing each other. Inhale with belly breaths as you press your palms together tightly. Exhale gently while you separate your palms and place them in your lap. Repeat three to five times until you feel your body is calm.

- Any other quick calming technique you already use, perhaps squeezing a stress ball or silent self-talking of a sentence such as "I am in control."

Note: The next sections present scenarios for you to practice with your elementary, middle, high schoolers, and even college students. If you feel creative, brainstorm as a family, and feel free to create your own scenarios.

For a few of the scenarios that follow, we will offer possible action, suggestions of what your sons and daughters could do. With these solutions as models, we're confident that you will not hesitate to use your T. E .A.M. thinking to solve the other scenarios.

ACTIVITY: Elementary Student UPstander Scenarios (E)

Scenario 1: Jewish Physical Features
At fourth-grade outside recess, you notice one boy is shooting a basket into the hoop. Two other boys run by. One points at the shooter's face and shouts, "Hey, look! A two-fer—big Jew nose and Jewfro" and continues running.

As an Upstander, what could *you* do?

Background information: Physical stereotypes of Jews have existed since the thirteenth century. Often, Jews were described and drawn as being hairy with large, hooked noses, yellowish-brown skin, and dark beady eyes. During medieval European times, Jews were portrayed as having boils, warts, and other deformities. Caricatures and cartoons of Jews with exaggerated or misshapen facial features continued in succeeding centuries. During the 1920s–40s, the Nazis used different forms of propaganda to present Jews as less than human or as disfigured humans. "Jewfro" entered the vocabulary in the 1950s. It refers to the excessively tightly curled hair of some Jews.

Possible Action : You take a deep breath. You decide to use the immediate strategy "Walk the person away." You walk toward the boy who is the target, in an assertive manner. You make direct eye contact and speak clearly and confidently, holding a tennis ball in one hand, "Hey, come on, let's have a catch out in the field."

Scenario 2: Love of Money

Your younger sister and her best friend have decided to bake cookies together to give to their teacher on her birthday. They've asked you (you are in fifth grade) to help them. They show you a list of ingredients they need to purchase.

"Let's go online and write down the cost of each ingredient," your sister suggests. "Then we can each pay half of the total cost."

"I'm OK with the cost list," says the friend. "But all you Jews are so good with money; you figure out the cost for both of us."

As an UPstander, you realize that the friend has not complimented your sister, but made a stereotypical remark. What could *you* do?

Background Information: In earlier centuries in many countries, Jews were not permitted to become landowners or earn a living in numerous occupations. In the Middle Ages, the only options Jews had were in trade, commerce, or money-lending at interest, a job from which Christians were prohibited by the Church. Naturally, some but not all of these Jewish moneylenders became wealthy.

* * *

A creative, thoughtful, and accomplished people such as the Jewish people should be known by what they have done and not by what has been done to them.

—**Deborah Lipstadt,** Ambassador, U.S. Special Envoy to Monitor and Combat Antisemitism

ACTIVITY: Middle School/High School UPstander Scenarios (MS/HS)

Scenario 1: The Devil

This is drawn from a true story. Harlene's daughter Pamela, then a high school freshman, was adjusting to the family's move to a new community. Her sense of loss of her tight group of friends from her old neighborhood was a constant, but she was determined to try to cope with what she called "my worst nightmare." On her third day in her new high school, she had just joined the lunchroom line to pick up a tray when five guys formed a circle around her. One whispered, "Hey Jew-girl, I really like your hair—nice horns." Another tapped her shoulder, smirked, and commanded, "Spin around so we can see your forked tail."

Possible Action: If you were the target, you calm yourself. You decide to use the later strategy "Have a talk with the offender." Because you are not totally comfortable with talking with the five guys yourself, you ask two friends, Jeff and Aaron, to go with you to the table where the five are sitting together. You stand in an assertive manner, look at the five directly and say clearly and confidently with a calm expression on your face, "Help me understand what you meant by "nice horns" and "forked tail".

If you had overheard this exchange as an UPstander, what could *you* do?

Background information: Claiming the Jew is the devil has been a form of antisemitism for thousands of years. Even today, individuals refer to the John 8:41–44 in the New Testament where Jesus says to his fellow Jews: "For you are the Children of your father, the devil, and you love to do the evil things he does."

Scenario 2: "Holocough" and Poisoning the Well—Blaming Jews for COVID-19
You see this meme on Facebook "Holocough—If you have the bug, give a hug. Spread the flu to every Jew." It connotes that Jews are spreading COVID to hurt the Palestinians.

On X (formerly known as Twitter), you receive this message: "Jews are poisoning the well again with COVID. It connotes that they benefit from sales of the vaccine."

As an UPstander, what could *you* do?

Background information: For centuries, Jews have been blamed for disease spreading as well as for profiting from disease medications. In the fourteenth century, Jews were accused of causing the bubonic plague by spreading the germs through common drinking wells; thousands of Jews were murdered as a result. In the 1890s, American Jews were blamed for the outbreak of tuberculosis. In the 1930s, Hitler accused Jews of being vermin and spreading bacteria.

Scenario 3: The ((( ))) Symbol

In an article in your local weekly newspaper about the successful opening of a new restaurant, ((( ))) appears around the owner's name: "The new restaurant owner (((Max Rosenberg))) . . . ".

As an UPstander, what could *you* do?

Background information: This symbol is used by antisemites, neo-Nazis, and white nationalists to highlight the names of Jewish individuals or organizations owned by Jews. In their view, this "echo" symbol represents the supposed damage caused by Jewish people that reverberates from decade to decade.

Scenario 4: Jewish Lightning—Greed

Your evening TV news coverage highlights a devastating fire that burned a nearby bowling alley to the ground. A three-minute video of comments from on-the-scene observers was included. One of the most forceful comments was: "How intolerable! This is clearly an undeniable case of Jew lightning. Katz, the building's owner, should be sentenced to jail for the rest of his worthless life."

As an UPstander, what could *you* do?

Background information: For centuries, a percentage of Jews have been property owners. Often, fires would occur, and gossiping individuals would opine that because of their greed, the Jewish owners had set their own buildings on fire to collect the insurance money. This alleged practice was often spoken of as "Jewish lightning." Use of this descriptor was almost as common as "jewing them down" (bargaining unscrupulously for a lower price).

Scenario 5: The Antisemitic Meme

On your cell phone, you see a meme created or passed on by one of the students in your school: a caricature of an elderly Jewish man with a large nose, saying Hitler should have killed all the Jews.

As an UPstander, what would *you* do?

Possible Action: Take a screenshot and share it with an adult, your teacher, parent, or a trusted adult.

Background information: For centuries, stereotypes and tropes have existed for the Jewish people. Taking action in your school means this kind of biased representation is not acceptable. If you can share this confidentially with your school teacher or counselor, perhaps they can contact the student's family and ask them to take the hurtful meme down.

Activity: Make up some scenarios of your own *or* ask your kids what has happened to them or their friends.

ACTIVITY: Being a Courageous UPstander
These four categories can be alike and different.

- How are they alike?
- And how are they different?
- How do they intersect?

1. Standing up for Jewish *self*—identity and pride

2. Standing up for *others*—whether Jewish or not

3. Standing up for *Jewish people*

4. Standing up for *Israel*

Young people have a real opportunity to shape the post-COVID world. Not in a cowardly way, hidden behind screens or disguised by large crowds, but by taking an active role, speaking up, and engaging in dialogue with more senior decision-makers.
—**Vanessa Hites,** Jewish Diplomatic Corps of the World Jewish Congress (Chile)

Social Media

There is a deluge of antisemitism on social media. Please discuss the challenges and solutions with your family. Tell them you are aware and you want to T.E.A.M. with them to respond safely to protect not only them, but other Jewish children and teens as well.

ACTIVITY: Media Literacy, Social Media and Reporting Antisemitism as an UPstander

What is media literacy? First, let us tell you what it is not. It is not managing your family's media and learning how to be more technologically advanced. It is not downloading the most apps. Here is the definition from the National Association of Media Literacy Education: "the ability to access, analyze, evaluate."

Don't we want this for all our children? Media literacy is a tool to create independent, analytical thinking—one of the foundations for UPstanders. Media literacy teaches children to be analytical media consumers. It teaches ethics and instructs them how to analyze media, advertising, news, and social media. It helps them to distinguish the truth from fiction, encouraging them to learn fact-checking.

It drills down on propaganda (so relevant, important, and scary today) and explains the hazardous consequences of propaganda's slippery slope into misinformation, falsehoods, stereotypes, myths, sexism, racism, and violence.

ACTIVITY: UPstanding Tactics for Social Media

In addition to a diversity appreciation deficit, social-emotional skills for our youth are declining at a precipitous rate. Why? Because of too much media, a lot of it being false, misleading, and cruel.

Antisemitism is a pervasive problem on most social media, including Instagram, Facebook, and TikTok, through videos as well as attacks on Jewish content creators. Common antisemitic conspiracies portray Jewish people as money-grubbing, controlling the media and banks, and manipulating politics. Videos show blood-libel tropes, antisemitic caricatures, Holocaust denial, and glorification of both Hitler and Nazis.

This is a perfect time to employ the T.E.A.M. concept—parents working together with their kids and teachers working with their students. Let them know that social media, memes and fake news can be harmful to them, their friends and their peers. Coach your kids/students to take screenshots and report to the school, to you, or to another trusted adult. Practice doing just that.

On the internet and in social media, *bad actors* and influencers are setting traps of name-calling, provocative memes and fake news. They are looking for reactions. Advise youth *not* to respond and engage. Instead utilize the T.E.A.M. concept to confirm that you care and create receptive conversations with your kids. Show them you are listening and are there to brainstorm solutions together.. like a real T.E.A.M.

Great resources like protectingkidsonline.org and counterhate.com are listed in the Resource section and on the Jewishupstanders.org website. Visit these and other sites with children and teens; an exploration together will get the conversation going while piquing their curiosity.

There is some good news. Young Jews are pushing back on social media. Looking for pro-Jewish accounts to follow? Or maybe create your own? Here are a few:

X

@yourjewishlife

@blackjewishmagic

@jewishoncampus

TikTok

@therealmelindastrass

@sj_rachel

@frumjewishblackboy

@adielof

Little Jewish UPstanders grow into big Jewish UPstanders.
—Lynne Azarchi

We feel strongly that knowledge of media literacy should be mandatory for every Jewish parent, teacher, and principal. It's not rocket science, and we hope we have convinced you of its critical importance and rightful place in your home.

CULMINATING ACTIVITY: If I Had a Magic Wand (finish the below sentences):

- Jews would …

- All people would …

- Other religions would …

- My friends would …

- My Jewish friends would …

- My family would …

- I will …

- For myself, I can and will …

- For others, I can and will …

- For the Jewish people, I will …

- **Signed** _____
  Date _____

This is like a mini-contract. May your commitment be binding.

Final Thoughts

We choose to close this Activities section with hope. The Hebrew word *tikvah* means "hope." It comes from the root *kav*, which means "thread" or string."

We reflect on the fact that our Jewish faith is the oldest spiritual tradition of the Western world. While the thread of hope at Judaism's core has often frayed throughout thousands of years of being attacked by hate, bias, tropes, and discrimination, the Jewish people's acts of bravery, courage, and lovingkindness have always carefully repaired the tear and strengthened hope anew.

If we continue to behave as bystanders and teach our children how to be bystanders, we will be in the same place in fifteen to twenty years. We must be UPstanders.

We hope we have inspired you to believe that if we teach our children and students both pride and empowerment, we can better interrupt and disrupt hate, bias, and discrimination not only for Jewish children, but for all youth.

We, as adults, have a responsibility to role model courage and persistence in building a culture of repelling and reporting antisemitism and bias; this Guidebook is designed to help parents, grandparents and teachers. Then, when our children are college students and adults, they will have a better chance of commanding more kindness and respect, and living openly and proudly with others as Jews.

If more of us take the challenge, perhaps the next generation can make a significant contribution to reducing antisemitism and bias for all children. The world can be better and different—if we start now.
Time is a precious thing. Never waste it.
—**Gene Wilder,** Jewish actor

As we honor our ancestors' resilience in the face of adversity, let us affirm that it is now our responsibility to step up and defend our people and our values.
—**David Harris,** former American Jewish Committee CEO

Part Three

Quiz—True or False

1. Antisemitic incidents are rising for youth, especially in the last six years.

2. Most antisemitic incidents are unreported to schools and the police.

3. There is not much we can do about antisemitism.

4. Antisemitic incidents harm both targets and bystanders who observe the incidents.

5. The most important thing parents and teachers can do to fight antisemitism is practice various strategies with their children, teens, and students.

6. Antisemitism can adversely influence a child's self-esteem.

7. A strong sense of ethnic identity and religious orientation make for the best UPstanders—those who "stand up and speak out."

8. A Jewish home that values kindness and diversity fosters youth that lean toward social and racial justice.

9. Antisemitism intensified in the Middle Ages.

10. Family conversations about antisemitism should start in middle school.

11. Over the last decade, the Holocaust is being discussed less in schools around the country.

12. Empathy (walking in others' shoes) is an important step that precedes empathic action.

13. Jewish heroes inspire youth and are great role models.

14. A family can be a great team to work together to fight antisemitism.

Answers are on the Jewishupstanders.org website

Part Four

Reporting—Why Bother?

We have shared that most of us act like bystanders, afraid to "stand up and speak out." Thousands of antisemitic and bias crimes and incidents are *not* reported. Some adults, kids, schools, and communities are fearful of drawing attention to themselves. Others are brave but do not know where to report.

Why should *you* report? Because you are role modeling for your children, friends, and neighbors that you are taking an active role to highlight a problem that must be addressed. A report tells the school, police, and FBI that we have a problem in the community that demands immediate attention. It is critical for Jews that an accurate assessment of antisemitism be tallied, shared, and discussed so all of us can look bias straight in the face and attack the causes and roots of tropes, discrimination, and stereotypes. When you report, you become a part of the proactive system to stop hate and bias.

Hate incidents vs. hate crimes

First, let's understand the definitions.

A **hate crime** is a crime against a person, group, or property motivated by the victim's real or perceived protected social group. You may be the victim of a hate crime if you have been targeted because of your actual or perceived: (1) disability, (2) gender, (3) nationality, (4) race or ethnicity, (5) religion, (6) sexual orientation, or (7) association with a person or group with one or more of these actual or perceived characteristics. Hate crimes are serious crimes that may result in imprisonment or jail time.

A **hate incident** is an action or behavior motivated by hate but that, for one or more reasons, is not a crime. Examples of hate incidents include:

- name-calling

- insults

- displaying hate material on your own property

- posting hate material that does not result in property damage

- distribution of materials with hate messages in public places

The Constitution allows hate speech as long as it does not interfere with the civil rights of others. While these acts are certainly hurtful, they do not rise to the level of criminal violations and thus may not be prosecuted. However, it is important to note that these incidents have a traumatic impact on the victims as well as on the community at large.

Hate incidents as defined above should be reported to schools, synagogues, municipalities, and appropriate agencies.

Where to report

The best site we recommend to orient yourself about reporting would be AJC's website: Search: "Reporting Antisemitism."

Here is some sage advice from Lynne's friend Philip Sellinger, U.S. Attorney for the District of New Jersey: "We recommend reporting to multiple law enforcement agencies. First, call the police or 911. They are the first responders and will be positioned to respond quickly. We then suggest you contact those federal and state law enforcement agencies—starting with the FBI and any state's U.S. Attorney's office."

Combating Hate Crimes: Where to Report

- Federal Bureau of Investigation: 1 800-CALL-FBI or tips@fbi.gov

- U.S. Attorney's Office—Civil Rights Division in your state

- U.S. Department of Justice—Civil Rights Divisions, Washington, D.C.

- Division on Civil Rights office in your state

- Division of Criminal Justice office in your state

Practice, practice, practice

Why not practice reporting with your family? Consider scenarios and role-playing. In many cases, you can report anonymously to protect your privacy. **If this is a safety issue or emergency, immediately dial 911.**

Note: These recommendations about reporting also apply to other marginalized groups that experience hate incidents and hate crimes.

Part Five

Resources

Note to readers: For a more updated Resource section with links, please visit Jewishupstanders.org

National Jewish Organizations

American Jewish Committee (ajc.org)

> "No Jew in the U.S. –or anywhere in the world–
> should feel unsafe expressing their Jewish
> identity . . . Fear of antisemitism is affecting how
> too many American Jews conduct their daily lives..
> whether they feel comfortable publicly identifying
> as Jewish . . . whether they feel safe in their own
> country. For young Jews, the data paints an even
> more somber picture."
> **– Ted Deutch,** AJC Chief Executive Officer

Advocating for the Jewish people and Israel. Defending democratic values for all. With more than 30 offices worldwide, plus partnerships with 37 international Jewish community organizations, the American Jewish Committee (AJC) is making a difference on the issues that matter. The challenges facing the

Jewish people are great. They demand a response from an organization with global reach and impact.

AJC The State of Antisemitism in America 2022

Nine in ten American Jews believe that antisemitism is a problem in the United States. Eight in ten believe it has increased in the past five years. Jews' concerns align with FBI data, which show increased levels of antisemitism in the United States.

AJC Leadership Program for High School Students

Today's high school students are tomorrow's Jewish leaders. Leaders for Tomorrow (LFT), AJC's education and advocacy program for teens, empowers young Jews to speak up for Israel and the Jewish people.

LFT helps high school students develop a strong Jewish identity and trains them as advocates for Israel and to be voices against antisemitism. LFT gives students the tools to talk about the issues impacting world Jewry today and the confidence to stand up for these issues in college and throughout their lives, no matter how difficult the situation.

AJC Disrupt Antisemitism for Young Adults

What a great idea. AJC inaugurated a nationwide award for young adults pushing back against antisemitism. Here are the five winners of AJC's 2021 Disrupt Antisemitism Youth. Get inspired and visit these websites to observe young adults taking a stand against antisemitism.

1. The Inter-Community Youth Initiative

Conceived of by students from **Yeshiva University Los Angeles High School (yula. edlioschool.com)**, brings Jewish and non-Jewish high school students together for a fellowship program designed to build trust, foster understanding, and fight antisemitism and racism.

2. Jew or False (www.jeworfalse.com)

A digital content series designed to fight antisemitism. Presented in the style of a satirical news show, Jew or False fights Jew hatred, inspires Jewish pride, and corrects misinformation on issues important to the Jewish community.

3. New Zionist Congress (www.newzionists.org)

The goal of **New Zionist Congress (www.newzionists.org)** is to combat the rising tide of anti-Zionism in youth-centered spaces. According to AJC's recently released *State of Antisemitism in America* report, over 80 percent of both Jews and the U.S. general public consider anti-Zionism—as represented by the statement "Israel has no right to exist"—to be antisemitic. New Zionist Congress organizes young Zionist Jews and their allies to stand up for Jews, wherever they are from.

4. Olive Branch Pictures (www.olivebranchpictures.org)

A comic and animation studio that fosters mutual understanding between Israelis and Palestinians. Olive Branch is producing a film and graphic novel called *Shira and Amal* about an Israeli girl and a Palestinian girl who learn to cope with the traumatic loss of loved ones by escaping into the world of music.

5. Uri L'Tzedek (utzedek.org)

An Orthodox social justice organization guided by Torah values and dedicated to combating suffering and oppression. Uri L'Tzedek takes on antisemitism in progressive spaces by conducting workshops with its partner organizations on what antisemitism is, how it manifests, and how to combat it.

AJC's Translate Hate Glossary can be downloaded online—visit ajc.org

Anti-Defamation League (adl.org)

In 1985, the Anti-Defamation League (ADL) launched a "World of Difference" campaign to be the leading provider of anti-bias education in North America. These resources have been used by schools, universities, corporations, law enforcement agencies, and community organizations.

Here are some basics from the ADL:

What is the difference between anti-Semitism and anti-Zionism?

Anti-Zionism is the opposition to Israel as a Jewish state. When criticism of Israel makes use of anti-Semitic stereotypes, blames all Jews for the actions of that country's government, or uses coded terms like "Zionist" to describe a Jewish person in general, criticism crosses the line into being anti-Zionist.

Is Holocaust denial a form of anti-Semitism?

Holocaust denial is a type of antisemitic propaganda that emerged after World War II and uses pseudo-history to deny the reality of the systematic mass murder of six million Jews by the Nazis and their allies during World War II. Holocaust deniers generally claim that the Holocaust never happened, or that a much smaller number of Jews died but primarily due to diseases like typhus. They also claim that legitimate accounts of the Holocaust are merely propaganda or lies generated by Jews for their own benefit.[35]

BBYO (bbyo.org)

BBYO (formerly B'nai B'rith Youth Organization) is the leading pluralistic Jewish teen movement, aspiring to involve more Jewish teens in more meaningful Jewish experiences. As expressed in its core values, BBYO welcomes Jewish teens of any background, denominational affiliation, gender, race, sexual orientation, or socioeconomic status, including those with a range of intellectual, emotional, and physical abilities.

With a network of hundreds of chapters across North America and in 60 countries around the world, BBYO reaches nearly 70,000 teens annually and serves as the Jewish community's largest and most valuable platform for delivering fun, meaningful, and affordable experiences that inspire a lasting connection to the Jewish people.

HIAS (hias.org)

HIAS (formerly the Hebrew International Aid Society) provides legal and social services to immigrants, refugees, and asylum seekers from all over the world. Its slogan is "Welcome the stranger—protect the refugee."

Israel Forever Foundation (israelforever.org)

The Israel Forever Foundation is an engagement organization that develops and promotes experiential learning opportunities to celebrate and strengthen the personal connection to Israel as an integral part of Jewish life and identity.

JDC (jdc.org)

The JDC (formerly American Jewish Joint Distribution Committee) has been a leading Jewish humanitarian organization since 1914.

Jewish Community Public Affairs (jcpa.org)

Jewish Community Public Affairs (JCPA) is committed to bringing together the organized Jewish community. It brings together Jewish Community Relations Councils and 16 national Jewish organizations to tackle pressing issues of the day, build consensus, and work in common cause with diverse partners in the public square.Inspired by Jewish values of human dignity and equal justice under the law and an abiding commitment to vibrant and secure Jewish communities here, Israel and throughout the world, JCPA convenes and catalyzes its network to work with public officials and build deep relations and engage in advocacy coalitions based on shared goals with other civic, racial, ethnic and faith-based leaders and communities.

JCPA has been the organized national Jewish community's convener, intergroup connector, and policy advocate since 1944. Their motto is: educate, advocate, and mobilize.

Jewish World Watch (jww.org)

Jewish World Watch is an expression of Judaism in action, bringing help and healing to survivors of mass atrocities around the globe and seeking to inspire people of all faiths and cultures to join the ongoing fight against genocide.

Simon Wiesenthal Center (wiesenthal.com)

The Simon Wiesenthal Center confronts antisemitism and hate, promotes human dignity, defends democracy and freedom, and teaches the lessons of the Holocaust for future generations.

A report written and prepared by its research department through its Digital Terrorism & Hate project, *Holocaust Denial and Distortion on Social Media*, highlights the rise of Holocaust distortion and denial online. It demonstrates how memes and jokes about the Holocaust are commonplace on social media, with many of them popular with young people, leading to the proliferation of antisemitism and bias online.

Union for Reform Judaism (urj.org)

Amid an alarming rise in antisemitic rhetoric and violence, the Union for Reform Judaism has joined with the ADL in the creation of a multifaceted partnership.

Volunteers for Israel (vfi.org)

On your next trip to Israel, consider a few days of giving back and volunteering. Volunteers for Israel adult programs, offered year-round, give an insider's view of Israel. You will work alongside soldiers, base employees, and other volunteers on an Israel Defense Forces base, performing noncombat civilian support duties such as packing medical supplies, repairing machinery and equipment, building fortifications, and painting and maintaining the base. Lynne's cousin Barbara did this with her husband; they really enjoyed their experience.

Other organizations

- **American Jewish World Service (ajws.org)**

- **Facing History & Ourselves (facinghistory.org)**

- **Louis Brandeis Center (brandeiscenter.com)**

- **The Shoah Memorial (memorialsdelashoah.org)**

- **Stand with Us (standwithus.com)**

- **Stand Up to Jewish Hate (standuptojewishhate.org)**

A Tip for Searching for Websites

Instead of asking you to type in long links, search the words below:

- "Talking to your kids about antisemitism"

- "How to talk to your kids about antisemitism"

CALL, the Campus Antisemitism Legal Line, is staffed by a team of volunteer lawyers and overseen by Hillel International, the Anti-Defamation League, the Louis D. Brandeis Center for Human Rights Under Law and Gibson, Dunn & Crutcher LLP. Students, parents, faculty members and staff can report an incident online or by texting "CALLhelp" to 51555 legal-protection.org.

Books

- *Anti-Bias Education for Young Children and Ourselves* by Louise Derman-Sparks and Julie Olsen Edwards. This book offers practical guidance to early childhood educators (including parents) for confronting and eliminating barriers of prejudice, misinformation, and bias.

- *Antisemitism: Here and Now* by Deborah Lipstadt, U.S. Special Envoy to Monitor and Combat Antisemitism

- *Changing the World from the Inside Out—A Jewish Approach to Personal and Social Change* by David Jaffe

- *The Empathy Advantage: Coaching Children to be Kind, Respectful, and Successful* by Lynne Azarchi with Larry Hanover. Visit empathyadvantagebook.com.

- *Empowering Bystanders in Bullying Prevention* by Stan Davis with Julia Davis

- *Fighting Contemporary Antisemitism: From High School Textbooks to the Halls of the Capitol* by Rose Clubok

- *I Am Jewish: Personal Reflections Inspired by the Last Words of Daniel Pearl* by Ruth Pearl

- *Jewish Pride: Rebuilding a People* by Ben M. Freeman

- *The Oys and Joys of Parenting* by Maurice J. Elias, Ph.D. Elias is a professor in the Psychology Department at Rutgers University, director of the Rutgers Social-Emotional and Character Development Lab, and co-director of the Academy for Social and Emotional Learning in Schools.

- *Youth Voice Project: Student Insights into Bullying and Peer Mistreatment* by Stan Davis and Charisse L. Nixon

- *Heroes with Chutzpah* by Rabbi Kerry Olitsky https://heroeswithchutzpah.com/

Museums

- Anne Frank House (Amsterdam)

- Museum of American Jewish History (Philadelphia)Kidsbridge Youth Center (kidsbridgecenter.org)

- Museum of Tolerance (Los Angeles) (museumoftolerance.com)

- U.S. Holocaust Memorial Museum (Washington, DC) (ushmm.org)

- Museum of Jewish Heritage (NYC) exhibit: "Courage to Act: Rescue in Denmark" (mjhnyc.org)

  An extraordinary exhibition for children aged 9 and up telling the remarkable story of the rescue of the Danish Jews during the Holocaust. Themes of separation, bravery and resilience.

THE PITZALAHS

Free preschool and early elementary books, newsletters and resources, please visit pjlibary.org (Courtesy of the Harold Grinspoon Foundation and local Jewish Federations)

* * *

U. S. National Strategy to Counter Antisemitism (May 2023)
Main Points https://www.whitehouse.gov/wp-content/uploads/2023/05/U.S.-National-Strategy-to-Counter-Antisemitism.pdf

Part Six

Approaching the Principal, Counselor or Teacher After an Antisemitic Incident

As Lynne coached parents in *The Empathy Advantage: Coaching Children to be Kind, Respectful and Successful*:

This is hard for a lot of people. We get it. But if you have it in you to be a change maker, it can make all the difference. Lynne has done it, and so can you. It's easier if you don't go it alone. It is not only easier but more effective to gather a couple of other concerned parents to schedule a meeting with the principal or the school counselor. Start by asking your friends if they are passionate about this issue and, if so, to join you for a premeeting. Have coffee before the real meeting at the school and listen to one another.

Request a meeting. At your first meeting with the school staff person, be friendly and ask a lot of questions. Job One is to learn about the school's inventory of anti-bias programs, including antisemitism. What programs are they doing, what are they measuring, and what are they planning for the future? Don't be surprised if anti-bias programs don't exist; push for one. Harlene adds, based upon her three decades of being a public-school principal and meeting with concerned parents and guardians, that respectful inquiries are usually well accepted by administrators.

Regroup with your team and discuss what you've learned. Then perhaps as a team or just a committee, ask for a second meeting. Subsequent meetings could follow where you and your group encourage the school administrators to improve on antisemitism and other bias programs for all students. It takes a village, and we are anointing you—or your team. (A sample agenda for your meeting might be the three questions mentioned above; Lynne created the agenda to discuss these issues with her child's elementary school counselor.) When organized and steadfast, parents can be anti-bias drivers outside of the home and teachers can inspire caring classrooms and schools.

You might need to meet monthly and don't forget the bagels and cream cheese.

We have similar advice for teachers. In some schools, the principal and counselor might not be interested or feel they have time to focus on antisemitism and bias, stereotypes and hate. Find some allies to leverage "power in numbers" and see if that helps. [36]

Part Seven

Title VI of 1964 Civil Rights Act— Prohibits Discrimination

Overview of Title VI Title VI, 42 U.S.C. § 2000d et seq., was enacted as part of the landmark Civil Rights Act of 1964. It **prohibits discrimination on the basis of race, color, and national origin in programs and activities receiving federal financial assistance**.

Each U.S. Department has an Office of Civil Rights (OCR), including the Department of Education (DOE). Schools lose their funding when they do not address bias, discrimination and antisemitism.

Your students and kids are protected. If your child or student is enduring a hostile environment, and their learning is compromised, here are the steps:

1. Complain to your school counselor or principal. Hopefully they will respond. Document your complaint with a follow up email if you call. If no action is taken,

2. File a complaint with the DOE's OCR.

If a school does not take action and come into compliance, they are violating the law and can lose federal funds.

Upon receiving a complaint, DOE OCR officers investigate to determine if a school violated Title VI.

Please note: An OCR complaint must be filed within **180 days of the last act of discrimination.**

Many schools have internal/institutional grievance or complaint procedures. It is not required that an individual go through the internal process before they file an OCR complaint. However, if you choose to go through an internal process and you want to file an OCR complaint, you must file your OCR complaint within **60 days *after* the completion of the school's internal process.**

How to File

To ensure receipt of your correspondence, please consider emailing **(OCR@ed.gov)** or faxing (202-453-6012) it to our office, where it will receive immediate attention. If neither of these options are available to you, mail your correspondence to the address below, and we will process it as soon as conditions allow. You may also contact us at 800-421-3481 or **OCR@ed.gov** to confirm receipt of your correspondence.

U.S. Department of Education
Office for Civil Rights
Lyndon Baines Johnson Department of Education Bldg.
400 Maryland Avenue, SW
Washington, DC 20202-1100

DOE/OCR Discrimination Complaint Form

You do not have to use this form to file a complaint with the U.S. Department of Education's Office for Civil Rights (OCR). You may send OCR a letter or email instead of this form, but the letter or email must include the information in items 1-15 of this form. If you decide to use this form, please type or print all information and use additional pages if more space is needed. An online, fillable version of this form, which can be submitted electronically, can be found at: **http://www.ed.gov/about/offices/list/ocr/complaintintro.html.**

Appendix

BIASBUSTERS
JEWISH
Upstanders

UPstanders Against Antisemitism Programs

WORKSHOPS FOR PARENTS, GRANDPARENTS, AND RELIGIOUS SCHOOL EDUCATORS

Teacher Training ▪ Parent 'Circle' Workshops ▪ Keynotes ▪ Conference Speaker

Do Jewish youth know what to do when:

- THEY HEAR NAZI TAUNTS?
- NEGATIVE JEW JOKES ARE DIRECTED TO THEM OR THEIR FRIENDS?
- THEY OBSERVE VERBAL AND/OR NON-VERBAL SLIGHTS, SNUBS, INSULTS?
- THEY SEE ANTISEMITIC TROPES, CARICATURES, AND STEREOTYPES ONLINE?

Solution-Oriented — You will actively:

- Identify and discuss the challenges and problems
- Discover benefits of teaching identity, pride, and strategies to Jewish youth earlier
- Learn guidelines for creating a TEAM with your children/family in your home
- Gain understanding of & rehearse effective strategies your youth can use
- Roleplay scenarios to safely apply & practice the rehearsed effective strategies
- Receive pointers on how to work with public schools after/before an incident

In the Parents Circle, parents were very engaged and participating. I felt all of the adults, both parents and grandparents, were able to walk out with something to work toward to push back against antisemitism.

Sue Weiner, Education Director, Congregation Kol Emet

Workshops/ Teacher Training/Keynotes Available on Zoom and In-Person

The training program for our teachers was very beneficial; the UAA facilitator invited an open and honest conversation about the dilemma of our kids facing painful antisemitism. My teachers felt it was useful, learned new strategies and effective communication styles to teach our students confidence to safely address all bias.

Joan Hersch, Education Director, Congregation Brothers of Israel

Interested? Contact Lynne at lynne@biasbusters.net ▪ jewishupstanders.com

Bibliography

American Jewish Committee. *The State of Antisemitism in America 2022*. AJC Today newsletter, March 2023 https://www.ajc.org/AntisemitismReport2022.

Azarchi, Lynne, with Larry Hanover. *The Empathy Advantage: Coaching Children to Be Kind, Respectful, and Successful*. Lanham, MD: Rowman & Littlefield, 2020.

Davis, Stan, with Julia Davis. *Empowering Bystanders in Bullying Prevention*. Champaign, IL: Research Press, 2007.

Dweck, Carol. *Mindset: The New Psychology to Success.* New York: Penguin Random House, 2016.

Elias, Maurice J., Marilyn E. Gootman, and Heather L. Schwartz, *The Joys & Oys of Parenting: Insight and Wisdom from the Jewish Tradition*. Millburn, NJ: Behrman House, 2016.

Erikson, Erik H. *Identity: Youth and Crisis*. New York: Norton, 1968.

Freeman, Ben. *Jewish Pride: Rebuilding a People.* London: No-Pasaran Media, 2021.

Goldsmith, Marcelle, and Isabel Cohen. *Hands On. How to Use Brain Gym in the Classroom.* Ventura, CA: Edu-Kinesthetics, 2003.

Johnson, Paul. *A History of the Jews*. New York: Harper & Row, 1987.

Konrath, Sara H., Edward H. O'Brien, and Courtney Hsing. "Changes in Dispositional Empathy in American College Students Over Time: A Meta-Analysis." *Personality and Social Psychology Review* 15, no. 180 (2010): 180–198.

Lipstadt, Deborah E. *Antisemitism: Here and Now.* New York: Schocken, 2019.

Lipstadt, Emily A., and Nadine F. Marks. "Religious Social Identity as an Explanatory Factor for Associations between More Frequent Formal Religious Participation and Psychological Well-Being, *International Journal for the Psychology of Religion* 17, no. 3 (2007): 245–59.

Nansel, Tonja R. Mary Overpeck, Ramani S. Pilla, W. June Ruan, Bruce Simons-Morton, and Peter Scheidt. "Bullying Behaviors Among US Youth Prevalence and Association with Psychosocial Adjustment," *Journal of the American Medical Association* 285, no. 16 (2001): 2094–2100. doi:10.1001/jama.285.16.2094.

Neff, Kristin, and Christopher Germer. *The Mindful Self-Compassion Workbook: A Proven Way to Accept Yourself, Build Inner Strength and Thrive.* New York: Guilford Press, 2018.

Oliner, Samuel P., and Pearl M. Oliner. *The Altruistic Personality: Rescuers of Jews in Nazi Europe.* New York: Touchstone, 1992.

Schwartz, Barry L. *Jewish Heroes, Jewish Values Jewish Heroes, Jewish Values.* Millburn, NJ: Behrman House, 1996.

Southern Poverty Law Center. *Hate at School.* 2019. https://www.splcenter.org/sites/default/files/tt_2019_hate_at_school_report_final_0.pdf.

Spiro, Ken. *WorldPerfect: The Jewish Impact on Civilization.* Deerfield Beach, FL: Simcha Press, 2002.

Endnotes

1   "US hate crime highest in more than a decade—FBI," BBC, November 17, 2020, https://www.bbc.com/news/world-us-canada-54968498.

2   Southern Poverty Law Center, *Hate at School,* 2019, https://www.splcenter.org/sites/default/files/tt_2019_hate_at_school_report_final_0.pdf.

3   Anti-Defamation League, "U.S. Antisemitic Incidents Remained at Historic High in 2020," press release, April 26, 2021, https://www.adl.org/resources/press-release/us-antisemitic-incidents-remained-historic-high-2020.

4   Anti-Defamation League, *Audit of Antisemitic Incidents 2022,* March 23, 2023, https://www.adl.org/resources/report/audit-antisemitic-incidents-2022.

5   Ibid.

6   Ibid.

7   American Jewish Committee, *The State of Antisemitism in America 2022*, March 2023, AJC Today newsletter, https://www.ajc.org/AntisemitismReport2022.

8   American Jewish Committee Surveys of U.S. and Israeli Jewish Millennials, press release, April 25, 2022, https://www.ajc.org/news/american-jewish-committee-surveys-of-us-and-israeli-jewish-millennials.

9   Lynne Azarchi with Larry Hanover, *The Empathy Advantage* (Lanham, MD: Rowman & Littlefield, 2020), 6, 8.

10 Michael Lerner, "The White Issue: 'Jews Are Not White," *Village Voice,* May 18, 1993, https://www.villagevoice.com/the-white-issue-jews-are-not-white/.

11 Ben Freeman, *Jewish Pride: Rebuilding a People* (London: No-Pasaran Media, 2021), 11.

12 WebMD, "Types of Mental Illness," May 15, 2023, https://www.webmd.com/mental-health/mental-health-types-illness.

13 Erik H. Erikson, *Identity: Youth and Crisis* (New York: Norton, 1968).

14 Maurice J. Elias, Marilyn E. Gootman, and Heather L. Schwartz, *The Joys & Oys of Parenting: Insight and Wisdom from the Jewish Tradition* (Millburn, NJ: Behrman House, 2016), xiii.

15 Freeman, *Jewish Pride*, 9.

16 PJ Library is made possible through partnerships with philanthropists and local Jewish organizations and is a program of the Harold Grinspoon Foundation. Families raising children from birth through eight years old with Judaism as part of their lives are welcome to enjoy the free monthly benefits of PJ Library. Children ages nine through twelve can continue their Jewish journey by joining PJ Our Way.

17 Elias et al., Joys and Oys

18 Paul Johnson, *A History of the Jews* (New York: Harper & Row, 1987); Ken Spiro, *WorldPerfect: The Jewish Impact on Civilization* (Deerfield Beach, FL: Simcha Press, 2002).

19 Mark J. Perry, "Looking Back at the Remarkable History of the Nobel Prize from 1901-2020 Using Maps, Charts, and Tables," American Enterprise Institute, October 12, 2020,

https://www.aei.org/carpe-diem/looking-back-at-the-remarkable-history-of-the-nobel-prize-from-1901-2020-using-maps-charts-and-tables/.

20 Freeman, *Jewish Pride*, 187.

21 Freeman, *Jewish Pride*, xi.

22 Read more about this ongoing project at https://www.yadvashem.org/righteous.html.

23 Quote from Julian Powe, The Practice of Empathy," *Forbes*, September 11, 2012.

24 Kristin Neff and Christopher Germer, The Mindful Self-Compassion Workbook (New York: Guilford Press, 2018).

25 Carol Dweck, *Mindset: The New Psychology to Success* (New York: Penguin Random House, 2016).

26 Deborah E. Lipstadt, *Antisemitism: Here and Now* (New York: Schocken, 2019).

27 Emily A. Greenfield and Nadine F. Marks, "Religious Social Identity as an Explanatory Factor for Associations between More Frequent Formal Religious Participation and Psychological Well-Being, *International Journal for the Psychology of Religion* 17, no. 3 (2007): 245–59.

28 Samuel P. Oliner and Pearl M. Oliner, *The Altruistic Personality: Rescuers of Jews in Nazi Europe* (New York: Touchstone, 1992).

29 Michael Bond, "Where heroes come from—and how to become one," *NewScientist*, January 21, 2015, https://www.newscientist.com/article/mg22530050-700-where-heroes-come-from-and-how-to-become-one/.

30 Barry L. Schwartz, *Jewish Heroes, Jewish Values Jewish Heroes, Jewish Values* (Millburn, NJ: Behrman House, 1996), 94.

31 Freeman, Jewish Pride.

32 Elias et al., *Joys and Oys*, 171.

33 Everett Rattray, "Speaking Up Against Antisemitism and More," *Hadassah Magazine*, January/February 2022, 13.

34 Stan Davis with Julia Davis, *Empowering Bystanders in Bullying Prevention* (Champaign, IL: Research Press, 2007), 189–90.

35 ADL, "What Is… Anti-Israel, Anti-Semitic, Anti-Zionist?", https://www.adl.org/resources/tools-and-strategies/what-is-anti-israel-anti-semitic-anti-zionist

36 Lynne Azarchi with Larry Hanover, *The Empathy Advantage* (Lanham, MD: Rowman & Littlefield, 2020), 83-84.

Index

Acknowledgments

We are so appreciative of the support we received from people and organizations who have been addressing antisemitism, bias and stereotypes. Their contributions increased our vision, strengthened our activities, and affirmed our strong faith in the value of building the younger generation's skills in pushing back against the world's oldest hatred.

We are deeply grateful to Stan Davis for his research and guidance in dealing with bullying prevention as a system. Our thanks go to Rebecca Erickson, Marilyn Bellis and Marianne Alt and the facilitators at Kidsbridge Youth Center in Ewing, New Jersey for their anti-bias foundational work with youth on which we built strategies and methods. Another shout out to our local synagogue education directors, Jewish agencies and volunteers for their partnership on our youth antisemitism and genealogy programs.

We are grateful to Larry Hanover for his careful edit and preparing our endnotes. To our publisher, Maryann Karinch, our thanks for your support in recognizing that publishing a practical anti-bias resource for Jewish families was critically needed at this time.

We are indebted to 35,000 youth, parents and educators who shared their personal experiences of bullying, bias, exclusion and name-calling at Kidsbridge. It was upon this foundation of empathy and empowerment that we were able to *walk in their shoes* and be motivated to help *all* youth with strategies, skills and strengths to push back against bias, stereotypes and hate.

In conclusion, we express gratitude to our families and Jewish ancestors who battled to come to this country and create a safe place for their loved ones to thrive openly as Jews.

Printed in the USA
CPSIA information can be obtained
at www.ICGtesting.com
CBHW081904080424
6592CB00008B/21

9 781963 271072